E28

½

F.

Prayer and Providence

HULSEAN LECTURES FOR 1966

Prayer and Providence

A BACKGROUND STUDY

P. R. Baelz

Fellow and Dean of Jesus College
Cambridge

SCM PRESS LTD

LONDON

SBN 334 01284 8

First published 1968

© *SCM Press Ltd 1968*

*Printed in Great Britain by
Northumberland Press Ltd
Gateshead*

CONTENTS

PREFACE

CONTEMPORARY debate about the content of Christian belief can be as bewildering as it is exciting. The basic issues do not always stand out clearly. It sometimes seems as if the elusiveness of God is matched by the evasiveness of theologians. Nowhere is this more evident than when it comes to a discussion of prayer, especially prayer of petition and intercession. The sound we hear is uncertain. But prayer is the soul of Christian religion. A man's prayer is an index of his faith. The manner of his approach to God reveals his understanding of the manner of God's approach to man. What he expects of God reflects what he believes about God. The nature of his hope contains his doctrine of divine providence.

In these Hulsean lectures I have attempted to provide a framework within which discussion of prayer and providence may usefully take place. They might be described as an essay in reconciliation, for I have tried to bring together the apparently conflicting notions of God's transcendent being and immanent activity in the world, of man's religious dependence and responsible moral endeavour.

Christian tradition makes liberal use of the personal language of divine activity and purpose. Reflection on the mysterious being of God compels us to ask whether such language is to be taken seriously or whether it expresses a lingering but persistent anthropomorphism which needs to be radically discounted. Can anything be said in defence of retaining such personal analogies when impersonal analogies are to hand with so much to commend them? In what I have said I have tried to do justice to both kinds of analogy, but in the end I have returned to the language of personal being as fundamental to Christian experience and interpretation. I have argued that communion with God requires us to make room both for divine-human confrontation and for divine-human co-operation. Man exists before God and with God in the world. His prayer is a creative participation in divine activity. It is the extension of that initial apprehension by which he comes to acknowledge the being of God. In the final lecture I have tentatively suggested some of the implications of this view for our understanding of God's providence.

I freely confess that from time to time I have wondered whether I have been seeking to reconcile the irreconcilable, and whether the whole attempt has been misdirected. However, I have never finally convinced myself that this is so, and I have a strong suspicion that it is not so. In any case, even if the final judgment turns out to be that no such reconciliation is possible, I dare to hope that my efforts will not have been entirely wasted. A visible shipwreck may prove a salutary warning of submerged rocks to other navigators.

Let me end this brief introduction by quoting Blaise Pascal's profoundly suggestive thought, which seems to me to go to the heart of the matter: *'Dieu a établi la prière pour communiquer à ses créatures la dignité de la causalité'* (Pensées, 659).

I

Praying and Believing

A Hulsean lecturer is invited to lecture on 'some branch of Christian theology'. It may well appear that, in offering to treat of both prayer and providence, I have plainly over-reached myself, and that I should have been far more circumspect, not to say more modest, had I restricted my attention to one or other of these two great themes. Have we not here two separate branches of Christian theology, each meriting an independent and extended discussion? Was not my older and wiser friend right, when on learning the title to which I proposed to speak, he quietly remarked that both subjects were extremely difficult? Of the substantial truth of my friend's implicit warning I have no doubt whatsoever. My purpose, however, in linking the subjects together is to limit rather than to enlarge the field. Let me try to explain my meaning.

First, Christians affirm that the world in which we live and move and have our being in God's world, that it is the object of his care and concern, and that he is ceaselessly active in his work of creation and redemption. The temptation to ascribe the work of redemption to God but to let the world go to the devil has always been resisted by the main stream of catholic Christianity. Recurrent attempts to interpret the divine creativity in narrowly existential rather than widely cosmological categories, attractive as they are, have been generally rejected as a reduction of the total structure of Christian faith. God is Creator and Sustainer as well as Redeemer and Sanctifier. In the words of the collect for the Eighth Sunday after Trinity in the Book of Common Prayer, God's 'never-failing providence ordereth all things both in heaven and earth'.

Second, God invites men not only to believe in him and to call upon his name, but also to be his fellow-workers and to make their requests known to him in confidence that he will hear and answer them. They are to work and pray for the coming of his kingdom and for the provision of their own daily bread. They are to ask in the confidence that they will also receive. One of the gifts which Jesus Christ has made available to men is the gift of 'access to God with freedom, in the confidence born of trust in him'.[1] Such access is expressive of a new status of adoptive sonship. As sons they share both in their Father's love and in his work.

Now, both of these convictions seem to form a constitutive part of anything that may properly be called *Christian* faith. They embody the idea of a divine-human activity in the world. But how are we to understand and interpret this divine-human activity? How are we to spell out the relation between God's providence and man's prayer?

There is plenty of room here for discussion and for difference of opinion. It seems, on first thoughts, that we must be drawn in one of two equally uninviting directions, that we have a simple if bitter choice between Scylla and Charybdis. Either prayer is a vestigial survival from primitive magic, a sort of grumbling appendix to a reasonable Christian faith, such that the sooner it were removed the healthier the Christian body would be. Or it is a form of interior reflection and meditation, however elaborately it may be dressed up in the mythological robes of a dialogue between man and God. And what holds good of prayer holds good, *a fortiori*, of the Church's sacraments. The Eucharist, for example, must be either magic or memorial. No alternative interpretation is open to us. Neither prospect pleases, and it appears that there is no other.

If prayer were only a peripheral concern of Christian faith, this dilemma might be accepted as such without too much heart-ache. This, however, is not the case. Prayer is a touchstone of a man's

---

[1] Ephesians 3.13 (New English Bible).

religious beliefs. What he believes about prayer is an indication of what he believes about God. More particularly, what he does about prayer is an indication of what he believes about it. It might even be argued that there is, at least for the Christian, a logical connexion between belief and prayer—that where there is no prayer to God there cannot be any real belief in God. There might be some notional assent to the proposition that God exists, but this would not have the full force of what is intended by the phrase 'belief-in-God'. According to this way of thinking and speaking, prayer would not be a possible consequence of believing in God, but it would itself be an element in belief, so that someone who professed to believe in God but never prayed to God would be guilty of a kind of self-contradiction. We might say of such a person that he did not *really* believe in God, or that he had a different idea of God from the idea proper to Christian theology. Whichever course we adopted, we should be implying that it was logically impossible for him to believe in God and not to pray to God. To cease to pray would be to cease to believe. The point I am making is this. I am suggesting that in certain religious contexts, whatever may be the case in other contexts, it is possible to detect a necessary connexion between the concepts of belief and prayer—to the illustration and better understanding of both.

At this point we may perhaps be allowed a slight digression. That in a religious context two concepts, which are not normally related logically, can in fact have such a necessary relationship may be seen from a consideration of the notions of loving God and loving one's neighbour. It might be thought that these notions expressed separate and logically unrelated activities, and that the connexion between them was synthetic rather than analytic. Nevertheless, within a certain religious context it may be argued that 'loving one's neighbour' is part of what is meant by 'loving God'. As the first letter of John puts it: 'If a man says, "I love God", while hating his brother, he is a liar. If he does not love the brother whom he has seen, it cannot be that he loves God whom he has not seen.'[2] This, I suggest, is a *logical* 'cannot'. When Diana says 'You

[2] I John 4.20 (NEB).

cannot love me if you do not love my dog', she may take my failure
to love her dog as a sign that I do not really love her, but the concepts of my love for her and my love for her dog remain logically
unrelated. Is there, however, such a complete logical disjunction
between love of God and love of neighbour? One hesitates to speak
in two breaths of loving God *and* of loving one's neighbour, just
in case it might be inferred from this manner of speaking that it
was conceivable to love God without loving one's neighbour. Hence
some writers have preferred to speak of loving God in one's neighbour or of loving one's neighbour in God. The activities are not
unrelated, nor are they identical. The one, as it were, includes the
other.

Let us now return to our own proper theme. The distinctively
religious character of a man's belief in God may be seen in his
belief about prayer. However, when we turn to consider prayer
itself we come face to face with all sorts of problems and difficulties.
It is notorious that every book on prayer has a chapter on its difficulties. These are both practical and theoretical. Even so, they all
stem from the one fundamental problem, namely, what prayer is.
Do we stand, sit, kneel or lie prostrate when we pray? Do we
pray when we feel like it, as if we were taking a glass of sherry,
or do we abide by prescribed hours, as if we were having a dose of
medicine? How do we begin to pray? These, and countless other
related questions, can be seen for what they are only when the
nature and purpose of prayer itself have been determined. In his
chapter on prayer in *Honest to God*, John Robinson remarks that
he found the traditional advice given to those learning to pray,
namely, to withdraw from the ordinary round of daily life and concentrate on the immediate presence of God, of little or no help, and
that for him prayer came alive only when he was so deeply involved
in the realities of the world and concerned with the problems
and perplexities of his fellow-men that he discovered he had penetrated through the world to the reality of God. Are these two ways,
then, simply two different approaches to one and the same destina-
tion, so that Peter may take the quiet road while John takes the
busy road? Or are the destinations themselves different, and is the

name given to the two different procedures, namely, prayer to God, at best analogical, at worst equivocal? Religious people are sometimes heard to remark, after a noticeable difference of opinion, that despite their disagreements they are all going the same way in the end. But are they? This sounds perilously like nonsense. What could it mean? Even if they are, how do they know that they are? What reason could be given for such pious optimism? Even supposing that it were in some queer way true, does it really make no difference of any importance by which road they choose to travel?

Clearly we must press our question concerning the nature and purpose of prayer. If we were to ask a mixed group of people to join together in prayer, what would they all do? More to our purpose, how would they interpret what they were doing? Would they all be doing the same thing, or at least sufficiently similar things, to justify the use of the single word 'prayer' to describe this behaviour? I once heard of a bishop who, in place of the more usual invitation, 'Let us pray', used simply to say, 'Kneel'. At least there could be no doubt what he expected from his congregation.

Let us be more specific. Suppose I were to ask my friends to pray for David Smith, who was undergoing an operation in a hospital at the other end of the land; or for Charles Brown, who was going out as a Christian missionary to Polynesia. What would they do? No doubt many of them would utter, aloud or to themselves, some such words as, 'God, help David Smith', or, 'God, be with Charles Brown'. But what account of their actions would they give to an inquirer who asked them what, exactly, they thought they were doing? Were they informing an all-knowing God of their desires and needs? Were they persuading an unchanging God to change the course of nature and history? Were they prompting an all-loving God to an act of mercy and loving-kindness? Or if they said they were laying bare the depths of their own being to the pervasive love of God, and in silent communion holding within this healing presence the one for whom they prayed, could this be anything more than a movement of the individual soul towards the divine, a flight of the alone to the Alone? When intercession is made, can God be said to *act*?

Christians are taught 'to make prayers and supplications on behalf of all men', but how are we to understand and interpret this activity of intercession? How does it fit in with our other workaday activities? What place has it in the picture of the world which we put together out of our non-religious experiences? It is no exaggeration to say that intercession provides a test-case for theological understanding. As H. Gollwitzer has written: 'It is no accident that with the effort to achieve a peace of partition between theology and modern world-views, the matter of intercessory prayer—consider only, for example, the discussions in Leibniz and in A. Ritschl—at once became a vicious question.'[3] At this point, as at no other, the believer finds himself behaving in a way which, in his more reflective moments, he suspects may be an indulgence either in magic or in wishful thinking. If it is theologically and scientifically preposterous to imagine that one can persuade God to change his mind and intervene in the ordinary course of events, what room is left for intercession, except perhaps as an *aide-memoire* for one's own future action?

What, then, is prayer? Numerous answers to this question have been suggested. Prayer is dialogue with God. Or it is practising the presence of God. Or it is the lifting up of heart and mind to God. These are only a few of the possible descriptions of the nature of prayer. I have selected these, however, in order to make two points.

First, they are all couched in language which is clearly analogical. What sort of dialogue is that between two parties, one of whom remains permanently invisible and silent? What sort of practice is the practice of the presence of God? Is it an activity which we cultivate and bring more and more under voluntary control, like practising to hold our breath? Or, again, is it possible for us to lift up our hearts by the same sort of deliberate determination as that by which we can pull up our socks? Clearly, these descriptions are only pointers, and until we have been given our bearings we shall

---

[3] Helmut Gollwitzer, *The Existence of God as Confessed by Faith*, London 1965, p. 53.

remain uncertain in what direction we are supposed to be looking.

The second point that I wish to make is this. All these three descriptions include the word 'God'. Now it would be possible to produce a definition of prayer which did not introduce the word 'God'. For example, 'prayer is the soul's sincere desire, uttered or inexpressed'. We might, then, continue to speak of prayer in a context from which belief in God was altogether excluded. Nevertheless, within a theistic context, such as I take to be that of Christian faith, the concepts of prayer and of God are logically related. Prayer is prayer *to God*, or it is not prayer at all. Consequently at the heart of all our difficulties concerning Christian prayer, both theoretical and practical, is the problem of understanding the being of God in general, and the relation of God to the world and to ourselves in particular.

The affirmation that prayer is prayer to God suggests that there is, or that there can be, some sort of relationship between ourselves and God. Now when we speak of a relationship, we normally speak of a relationship between two or more distinct terms, and in order to grasp the nature of the relationship we need to have some idea of the nature of the terms. We need at least to be able to isolate and identify the terms so that we can recognize them when reference is made to them. For example, any discussion of the nature of the relationship between Caesar and Cleopatra is bound to be obscure until it is known whether Caesar and Cleopatra are man and woman, or dog and cat. Or again, to take another celebrated example, nobody can begin to understand the relationship between a Cambridge College and Cambridge University until he realizes that the University is not another College-like entity, nor simply a collection of Colleges, but a corporate body the nature and function of which go to determine its relationship with the Colleges. However, when we consider the relationship between ourselves and God which is presupposed by prayer, we soon discover that at least one term in this relationship is consistently elusive—so elusive, in fact, that the question may well arise whether there are two distinct terms such that there can be a relationship between them. Perhaps prayer is simply a soliloquy, and the only relationship established in prayer is the sort of relationship that I can have with myself, as when I talk to myself, or despise myself, or laugh at myself.

I shall say nothing here about the other term in the relationship, namely, ourselves. But here too we are confronted with a certain elusiveness. Who am I? What am I? This very elusiveness, this sense of my being 'more' than any given momentary manifestation of myself, or indeed any series of such manifestations, this suggestion of self-transcendence, is precisely that feature in prayer which prompts the question whether we need to posit any other relationship than that which I can have with myself, or whether prayer is simply a reflexive activity, that is, an activity bent back upon myself.

It would appear, then, that we ought first to get our ideas straight about God, before we proceed to speak about prayer. But we have already seen that belief and prayer are not as easily separable as such a suggested procedure implies. A part of what we mean when we speak of God is that he is one to whom prayer is properly offered. The activity of prayer bears upon the content of belief. It may also bear upon the manner of believing.

In our own times no one has stressed the interdependence of belief and prayer more forcibly than Karl Barth, and I shall venture here to quote from him at some length. In his *Evangelical Theology*, he includes a chapter in which he discusses the intimate connexion between theology and prayer. According to him 'the first and basic act of theological work is prayer'.[4] This is not intended as a polite formality, like the Latin grace before hall dinner, nor even as a brief petition for God's help in the pursuit of theological truth. It is something much more fundamental. 'Theological work does not merely begin with prayer and is not merely accompanied by it; in its totality it is peculiar and characteristic of theology that it can be performed only in the act of prayer.'[5] No prayer, no theology!

Barth makes the following four points in elucidating his meaning. First, he refers to the peculiar epistemological status of the object of theological study. We cannot grasp it; it can only grasp us. That

[4] Karl Barth, *Evangelical Theology*, London 1963, p. 160.
[5] *Ibid*.

is, the proper object of theology, namely God, is not at our disposal, it is not a feature of our world which can be observed and pointed out in any detached manner. Nor can we do anything about this fact. On the other hand we need not on this account abandon theology. 'The knowledge that by our own powers nothing at all can be accomplished, allows and requires courageous action. Wherever theology becomes and remains faithful to its object, both God's grace and God's judgment, and consequently both the sinner's death and his salvation, must be taken equally seriously. In spite of all solitude and doubt, theology will be faithful to its object only and precisely when it allows itself to be tempted by it.'[6] The theologian can set his sails even if he cannot control the winds of heaven.

Second, we cannot take it for granted that when we are using the word 'God' we are in fact talking about God. We need to be continually illuminated by the divine light. 'Proper and useful theological work is distinguished by the fact that it takes place in a realm which not only has open windows (which in themselves are admittedly good and necessary) facing the surrounding life of the Church and world, but also and above all has a skylight. That is to say, theological work is opened *by* heaven and God's work and word, but it is also open *towards* heaven and God's work and word. It cannot possibly be taken for granted that this work is performed in this *open* realm, open towards the object of theology, its source and goal.'[7] Again, 'What theologian is there who is not continually surprised to find, even when he endeavours wholly and perhaps very seriously to press forward to relatively true and important insights and statements, that he is moving about in a human, all too human, circle like a squirrel in a cage? He may be listening more and more attentively to the witness of the Bible, and understanding more and more lucidly the confessions of faith, the voices of the Church fathers and of contemporaries, all the time combining these with the required openness to the world. As he lingers here and there on different occasions, he may, no doubt, come upon problems that are certainly interesting, or perceptions that are thought-provoking or even exciting. The only flaw is that the whole subject (and, as a

[6] *Op. cit.*, p. 159.   [7] *Op. cit.*, p. 161.

B

result, each particular topic as well) does not begin to shed light or to take on contours and constant features. . . . At such a moment he can and should turn exclusively towards the object of theology, himself, to God. But what else is such a turning to God than the turning of prayer?'[8] Barth goes on to describe this turning of prayer. 'Prayer begins with the movement in which a man wishes and seeks to win new clarity about the fact that "God is the one who rules". . . . Specifically, the question and inquiry about God will always demand and form a special activity. Other activities must retreat behind this one for a while (just as the activities of the week retreat behind the activity of the Sabbath). They do this just in order to be proper activities in their own right. They are disclosed and set in the proper light by prayer.'[9] Thus it is not only the nature of the theological object which calls the theologian to prayer. Theological activity itself can lose its ultimate sense and direction unless prayer is continually renewed.

Third, 'the object of theological work is not some *thing* but some *one*. . . . And He, this One, exists not as an idle and mute being for Himself, but precisely in this *work* which is also His *Word*.'[10] If man wishes to know God, he must hear God's word; and if he is to hear, he must listen. 'The task of theological work consists in listening to Him, this One who speaks through His work, and in rendering account of His Word to oneself, the Church, and the world. . . . For this reason all human thought and speech in relation to God can have only the character of a *response* to be made to God's word.'[11] It follows that 'human thought and speech cannot be *about* God, but must be directed *towards* God, called into action by the divine thought and speech directed to men, and following and corresponding to this work of God'.[12] Although theologians do in fact speak in the third person about God, such speech is 'a veil of theological thought', and after the manner of Anselm's *Proslogion* 'theological work must really and truly take place in the form of a liturgical act, as invocation of God, and as prayer'.[13] 'Any theology which would not even consider the necessity to respond to God personally could

[8] *Op. cit.*, pp. 161f.　　　　　[11] *Op. cit.*, pp. 163f.
[9] *Op. cit.*, p. 163.　　　　　　[12] *Op. cit.*, p. 164.
[10] *Ibid.*　　　　　　　　　　　[13] *Ibid.*

only be false theology. It would exchange what is real for what is unreal if it did not unfailingly keep sight of this I-Thou relationship in which God is man's God and man is God's man.'[14] Thus, theological thinking depends for its basic rationale upon the thinker's responses to One who engages him as person rather than as thing.

Fourth, theology can never assume that there are assured results of past theological reflection on which it is possible to build with perfect confidence for the future. The theologian's 'only possible procedure every day, in fact every hour, is to begin anew at the beginning'.[15] This derives from the fact that the theologian is dependent for the object of his study upon the free decision of that object, namely God, to make himself available. 'The ever-new start is the only possible way because the object of theology is the living God himself in his free grace. . . . Theological work cannot be done on any level or in any respect other than by freely granting the free God room to dispose at will over everything that men may already have known, produced, and achieved, and over all the religious, moral, intellectual, spiritual, or divine equipage with which men have travelled. . . . It is a fact that this work can be and is done with vigour only when it is done not in some sort of rearmament over against its object but in the undaunted disarmament and capitulation to its object—that is to say, in the work of prayer.'[16]

What are we to make of this? It may seem to some that we have lingered too long in the Barthian hot-house. We may be puzzled by the radically personalistic language in which Barth speaks of man's relationship to God. How far, we ask, does such language reflect the ontological structure of this relationship, and how far the psychological temperament of those who have a particular kind of religious experience engendered by a particular style of preaching? Barth writes almost as if God confronted man and spoke to him in very much the same sort of way as the preacher confronts his

[14] *Op. cit.*, p. 165.
[15] *Ibid.*
[16] *Op. cit.*, pp. 166f.

congregation and speaks to them from the exalted height of the pulpit. Some of us will remember with sympathy Austin Farrer's striking comment in *The Glass of Vision*: 'When Germans set their eyeballs and pronounce the terrific words "He speaks to thee" (*Er redet dich an*), I am sure, indeed, that they are saying something, but I am still more sure that they are not speaking to my condition.'[17] Again, we may wonder whether Barth's insistence on the radical freedom of God and on the consequent instability of the theological enterprise unless it is from moment to moment reconstituted by God's gracious self-disclosure does not suggest a God whose freedom borders upon an arbitrariness barely compatible with his wisdom and faithfulness. Despite these misgivings we may derive something of fundamental importance from Barth's exposition.

His use of personal categories and his emphasis on the freedom of God play an important part in our understanding both of the transcendence of God and of man's knowledge of God. It is characteristic of personal being at the human level that a man is not completely bound by his nature, that he has the freedom, limited though it clearly is, to transcend what the past has made him. Through this freedom he can exercise a certain creativity and claim a certain responsibility. He can give himself to other persons or he can withhold himself. Personal being, then, can provide us with an appropriate language with which to speak of the being of God. However, whereas man is bound to the world and only in a measure free, God is not bound to the world in a corresponding dependence. His freedom is absolute. The world is the object of God's creative activity but God does not, as man does, derive his being in any respect from the created world. The created world as such may disclose or it may conceal the presence of the creative God, but it discloses it only in so far as God chooses of his free grace to reveal himself. Thus the language of freedom and of personal relationship is used to reflect an ontological structure—to suggest a fundamental discontinuity between the being of God and the being of the world and at the same time to leave room for the possibility of man's coming to know God simply because God wills to make himself known.

[17] Austin Farrer, *The Glass of Vision*, London 1948, p. 8.

Prayer can then be seen as a serious attempt to prepare for God's gracious self-disclosure, and faith as the acknowledgment of this self-disclosure, an acknowledgment which is itself an expression of prayer—'My Lord and my God'.

These two related themes of the mode of God's transcendence and of the manner of man's acknowledgment of this transcendent God are so important for a proper understanding of the basic structure of prayer that I propose to say something further about each of them in turn.

Consider, first, the transcendence of God. It has often been remarked that Christian theology treads a perilous knife-edge between agnosticism and anthropomorphism. Certainly, an exclusive emphasis on the utter transcendence of God would seem to result in utter agnosticism, and such agnosticism is not to be held at bay by a few anthropomorphic sallies here or there, nor by a full-scale operation which turns theology into anthropology in the manner of Feuerbach and is in effect a form of atheism rather than of agnosticism. If, however, it should turn out that what is meant by the transcendence of God can best be adumbrated by the use of the categories of personal being, and by an emphasis on the freedom of God, then perhaps we can see why agnosticism and anthropomorphism are bound to threaten the theologian's attempts to speak about God. In speaking of the transcendence of God he is already using categories which have their root in his own being. Or, to put it in another way, the question about God cannot be raised without at the same time raising the question about man. But it is not the same question.

It might be argued that contemporary theological emphasis on the transcendence of God is in the first instance a development of the *via negativa*. We may be extremely cautious and hesitant in our assertions concerning what God is, but we are somewhat clearer in our minds concerning what God is not. Here we have learned both from theological criticism of nineteenth-century attempts to discover the being of God in and through some aspect of human consciousness and also from philosophical criticism of any analysis of assertions about God in terms of straightforward empirical assertions. God is not an object among objects in the observable world—not even a very powerful but peculiarly elusive object. If he were, he would, religiously speaking, be an idol. Philosophically speaking, his existence and behaviour would be subject to the ordinary rules of empirical verification. But if he is not an object among objects, what is he? Is he in any sense an 'object' at all? Is he in some sense 'beyond' the usual subject-object distinction? Or is he only an aspect of the human subject—a name by which we refer to our own hopes and fears, attitudes and policies, ideas and ideals? Is he only the World or Man writ large?

Barth's epistemological realism and theological objectivism are in part a massive attack on all attempts to reduce the being of God to that of the world or of man. God is other than the world and other than man. His being is hidden. There is a radical discontinuity between the being of God and the being of man. The impression left by this negative aspect of Barth's theology is one both of admiration and bewilderment. He seems to have achieved a far-reaching insight into what must be the case if God is to be God, and at the same time to leave everything hanging in the air. Either it is all tremendously real or else it is utterly meaningless. One is reminded of J. N. Findlay's assessment of the logical properties of the concept of God, that 'if God's existence is in any way *possible*, then it is also *certain* and *necessary* that God exists, a position which should give some comfort to the shade of Anselm'.[18] Either necessity or nonsense! How does one decide which? Presumably Barth would answer that the decision is not possible outside the context in which God discloses to us his own reality and in which we freely acknowledge it. The knowledge of God is an acknowledgment of his presence to us. It cannot be gained from any other source, nor in any other way. Without such acknowledgment, and apart from the attitude of prayer which accompanies such acknowledgment, we may well wonder whether our talk about God is anything but the completest nonsense!

Keeping in mind this fundamental question concerning the intelligibility of divine transcendence, let us now turn to the second

[18] J. N. Findlay, *Language, Mind and Value*, London 1963, p. 9.

of our two related themes, and take a further look at what I have called man's acknowledgment of God. Ever since Kant questioned the ability of the human mind to extend its categories of understanding beyond the objects of the phenomenal world, and, in his own words, 'found it necessary to deny *knowledge* in order to make room for *faith*', theologians have been tempted to adopt a non-cognitive analysis of the nature of faith. The greater the emphasis on God's transcendence, the greater the temptation to drive a wedge between believing and knowing. If God cannot be known, then faith-in-God is likely to be interpreted as faith in general, an attitude of trust and hope adopted in the face of the facts, itself ungrounded in fact of any kind. So faith creates God. The being of God is dependent upon human faith and has no reality outside this activity of faith. Faith is no longer the means by which the being of God is acknowledged, it is the power which brings God himself into being. Certainly this was not the Kantian understanding of faith, for in many important respects Kant remained a rationalist and a realist. Nevertheless, it is not, I think, altogether fanciful to find in Kant the beginnings of a movement of thought which, idealistic in its epistemology, prepared the way for just such a non-cognitive view of the nature of faith.

We must admit straightaway that a non-cognitive analysis of faith is not unattractive. For one thing, religious faith is certainly something more than an intellectual belief that certain assertions are true. It includes a measure of involvement, an element of personal decision and commitment. Belief without some kind of action consequential upon belief is barely belief at all. Faith without some kind of works is stillborn. Non-cognitive theories are right to stress this active element in religious faith. Furthermore, faith is peculiarly persistent. It frequently refuses to take things at their face value. It is apparently blind on occasions to the implications of the empirical evidence. It persists 'though the heavens fall'. It hopes against hope. This characteristic of faith certainly suggests that we are here dealing with attitudes rather than factual assertions, attitudes which may have their origin in human psychological needs without reference to any external state of affairs to which such attitudes may or may not be appropriate. Prayer, too, which, as I have suggested, is closely bound up with faith, has the same characteristic of persistence, and may be interpreted as the expression of a strong desire, a self-contained activity which requires no one to hear and respond to the prayer. 'The failure of prayer to bring about what was prayed for does not revise the belief in the power of prayer. The evidence is simply ignored.'[19]

Despite these considerations, however, there remains among most believers the conviction that their faith is well-grounded, that they have a reason for the hope that is in them, that their prayer is heard and that the heavens will not finally fall. They would express this conviction by the assertion that God is, and that he is faithful. Something of what is signified by his faithfulness is this 'fact' of his ultimate being.

If we take this conviction seriously, and ask what distinguishes it from an irrational obsession, the most likely answer that we shall receive is that it is given in and with what may perhaps be described as a non-inferential act of apprehension. It would, I think, generally be admitted that there is no straightforward inferential path by way of argument from what is not-God to God. An inference from the empirical to the transcendent is ruled out because the ordinary rules of inference are applicable only within the empirical world. The traditional 'arguments' are invalid as arguments. They may, however, express in the form of an argument what is really not an argument at all, but a fundamental act of apprehension by which the mind, starting from certain more or less general features of the empirical world, is brought to an awareness of that which 'transcends' the empirical world. The mind in this way 'grasps' a Reality to which it is on other occasions not alert.

The neo-Thomists are not the only philosophers of religion to stress this factor of non-inferential apprehension for any adequate analysis of men's acknowledgment of the reality of God. There are different ways of drawing attention to it and describing it. For example, H. D. Lewis argues that, when all that is irrelevant is

---

[19] Allen Wheelis, *The Quest for Identity*, p. 159. Quoted in P. Halmos, *The Faith of the Counsellors*, London 1965, p. 148.

cleared out of the way, the mind grasps the fact that there is a perfect Reality which is the ground and condition of the world of which we find ourselves a part. 'All that we encounter points to a Reality which is complete and self-contained and which is the ultimate ground or condition of all the conditioned, limited reality we find ourselves and the world around us to be.'[20] A consideration of empirical being leads to the rational apprehension of the fact that there is a transcendent being, perfect and complete in the way in which empirical being is imperfect and incomplete. In the last analysis, either we 'see' this to be the case, or we do not. There is no more ultimate or more general principle by an appeal to which we can prove it to be the case.

If H. D. Lewis provides us with an example of a quasi-rationalistic apprehension of the fact of God's existence, H. Gollwitzer provides an example of a more existentialist kind, in which an awareness of the reality of God is but one side of a coin of which the other is a self-commitment to the claims of God. In the case of God, 'knowledge and acknowledgment are one and the same act. . . . He who encounters us here is the One whose existence can be disputed only apart from the encounter . . . whose encounter at once throws us on our knees and calls out our worship, as is pictured in biblical scenes'.[21] The acknowledgment of God, the apprehension of his being, cannot occur apart from a confession of faith which is already an act of self-commitment. Now the question may be raised whether this way of speaking leaves sufficient room for the freedom of man's response. Is it possible, for example, for a man to rebel against God? It is instructive to compare here Gollwitzer's words with some of Barth's. Barth, while obviously sympathetic to an analysis of the knowledge of God which roots it in the insight and response of faith, is nevertheless anxious to preserve room for the freedom of man's response. 'To say that a person *must* believe would be inappropriate, since he can only really believe as a *free* believer, as one freed for faith. . . . This act is not a necessity but a permission granted man by God, consisting in the natural sequence and response by which

[20] H. D. Lewis, *Philosophy of Religion*, London 1965, p.144.
[21] H. Gollwitzer, *op. cit.*, pp. 126f.

man returns a bit of human gratitude for the grace shown him by God. Such faith is comparable to the natural development of a bud into a flower and the natural inclination of this flower towards the sun, or to the natural laughter of a child when he beholds something that gives him pleasure.'[22] We might make the point by saying that the acknowledgment of the being of God cannot be one of indifference. It is always accompanied by either a blessing or a curse.

Other writers have spoken in other ways about the structure of the basic act of religious apprehension. Some, like I. T. Ramsey, have compared it with 'pennies dropping' and our 'seeing' the point of something that has been said to us, or the 'light dawning' and our being confronted by a cosmic disclosure which is at the same time a disclosure of our own being. Others, like H. H. Farmer and John Baillie, have spoken of a 'sense' of the 'presence' of God, who 'confronts' us with an unconditional demand and promises us our final sustenance and succour. Others have preferred to use the language of hearing rather than of seeing. For example, in listening to the words of the Bible or of a sermon, we suddenly 'hear' the Word of God addressing us with judgment and mercy and calling for our obedience and response. In the main biblical tradition the language of faith is contrasted with the language of sight. In our present condition here and now we cannot, according to biblical thought, 'see' God; but we can 'hear' his commands and promises, and obedience will bring us to life and, at the consummation, to the vision of God. The language of hearing is, perhaps, more akin to the language of morality, and the language of seeing to the language of aesthetics. Religious language will no doubt include both, as faith is both cognitive and non-cognitive, both theoretical and practical; but moral language, with its insistence that all is not as it should be and that something must be done, is closer to the heart of that prophetic tradition which directs and dominates the religion of the Bible.

All talk of non-inferential apprehension must face the question whether it can have any claim to count as cognition. Now it is certainly the case that within any limited field of knowledge we

[22] K. Barth, *op cit.*, pp. 102f.

distinguish between knowledge and mere opinion by the application of various criteria of objectivity. Only those opinions which survive the test of these criteria are allowed to count as knowledge or as reasonable belief. When, however, we reflect at a deeper level upon the whole activity of knowing, we discover that the choice of our initial criteria, the decision what is to count as objective, even as real, is an activity which involves judgments of a different kind. At this level both subjective and objective factors are curiously interwoven. The drive to understand is a drive to make a personal and reflective response to that which confronts man in his whole being. It is a search for an *adaequatio reietintellectus*. In this search subjective judgments, decisions of relevance and significance, evaluations are all inescapable. But it would be a mistake to treat these judgments as if they were arbitrary presuppositions. Man can become aware of his presuppositions, and in becoming aware of them he can criticize them. Thus the drive to understand, the total cognitive activity, is itself a process both of apprehension and of criticism, and is directed towards a reality which both transcends and at the same time is patient of our limited modes of knowledge. It is this feature of our intercourse with what is other than ourselves which suggests the appropriateness of our using categories of personal intelligence to interpret the nature of that with which we have commerce. Such I take to be the insight enshrined in the teleological argument for the existence of God, even when the criticisms of Hume and others have been allowed their full force.

Returning to what I have called a non-inferential apprehension of God, we may summarize the drift of our present discussion of the relation between praying and believing in the following way. We apprehend God as himself apprehending us and ourselves as apprehended by him.

The acknowledgment of the reality of the transcendent God is like seeing something to which I had previously been blind. It is like hearing something to which I had previously been deaf. But the seeing and the hearing are aspects of an event which affect my whole being as a person. It is not possible to remain unconcerned: I must act. And unless I deliberately reject what I see and hear, I find myself responding to that which is revealed to me. My response is mine, and consequently it is free; nevertheless it is a response which is evoked from me and comes to me 'out of the blue'. I recognize it as a gift of grace, and not as an achievement of my own. I accept my own new being from the Being of God. I am in communion with God. I am participating in the life of God.

Let us call this activity of communion and participation the activity of worship or prayer. It is the deliberate response to that which has revealed itself to me and given me my new being. It is the activity by which this fundamental renewal is continued from moment to moment. It is an extended acknowledgment of God— recognition of his being, attention to his word, and self-surrender to his grace.

Prayer is thus an extension of faith. Faith is a moment in the activity of prayer. The acknowledgment of God in his transcendent being combines both believing and praying. In seeking to understand and master the world around us we make a definite break between the world and ourselves. We aim at objectivity. We keep ourselves as far as possible out of the picture. But in seeking to know God we cannot in this way exclude ourselves. We cannot know God from a distance. We know only as we are willing to be known. We apprehend only in so far as we ourselves are apprehended. We perceive only when we participate. It is to a consideration of this fundamental religious relationship of participation, or communion, that we must turn next.

II

Communion with God

UNLESS we are willing to concede that prayer is a self-contained activity like wishing, or dreaming, or holding one's breath, it seems *prima facie* plausible to think of it as a relationship between ourselves and God, and to suggest that a dispassionate consideration of the nature of both terms in the relationship would provide a useful preamble to further discussion of the relationship itself. We have seen, however, that the existence of God is not comparable to the existence of some object in the world, which might be observed and examined more or less dispassionately, or posited by hypothesis and established by prediction and experiment. God eludes an approach such as this. That is part of what is meant by the transcendence of God. He is known, if he is known at all, in an act of acknowledgment which is something like an intuition, something like the recognition of a moral command, something like a confession of trust and adoration. Thus belief in God and communion with God are not easily separable and cannot be treated in isolation from each other. It is this fact—namely, that we are ourselves personally involved in an acknowledgment of the being of God, and that this acknowledgment brings us not only to a new knowledge of God but also to a new knowledge of ourselves—which lends plausibility to the reductionist's view that 'knowledge of God' is nothing but self-knowledge and to the corollary that prayer is nothing but reflective meditation. It is impossible dispassionately to display God. It is impossible to refute the reductionist on his own ground. An acknowledgment of the reality of God will involve a change of ground, a fresh understanding of the being of oneself and of the world as well as an acknowledgment of that which transcends and gives reality to both.

If we cannot conduct experiments to prove or to disprove the existence of God, it would seem to follow that we cannot conduct experiments to prove or disprove the efficacy of prayer. Yet many believers are convinced that God does answer prayer, and that their experience has established the fact. Are we simply to brush their assertions aside on the grounds that they have ignored the occasions on which God has not answered their prayers, or that they are prepared to see any outcome as God's answer, whether it is affirmative or negative? Or is there a sense in which it is legitimate to say that the experience of prayer can justifiably be held to confirm the practice of prayer?

Certainly a totally impersonal approach is ruled out. It is ruled out on grounds which the believer himself should be the first to recognize as legitimate. God is not a mechanism to be set in action by a verbal shilling in the slot. If he were, he would not be God in the sense of the One who seeks to evoke above all else a man's obedience, love and devotion. He would be on a par with the impersonal world which is the object of man's mastery and manipulation. Prayer would no longer be communion, but a piece of applied science and the 'science' of prayer would be better studied in a college of advanced technology than in a seminary. If the question, 'What is the use of prayer?', means only, 'Does it produce the goods?', the questioner has abandoned the sphere of religion for that of the market-place.

If an allusion to popular song is not out of keeping with the high themes of our debate—and Bonhoeffer once remarked that 'absolute seriousness is not without a dose of humour'—we may venture to illustrate just such a view of the efficacy of prayer by reference to the song 'Santa Baby', unforgettably sung by Eartha Kitt. In this song, prayer is understood in straightforward terms of bargaining, and man's relation to God in terms of a contractual *quid pro quo*:

Think of all the fun I've missed,
Think of all the fellows that I haven't kissed;
Next year I could be oh so good
If you'll check off my Christmas list . . .
Come and trim my Christmas tree
With some decorations bought at Tiffany;
I really do believe in you—
Let's see if you believe in me.

If popular song is regarded as an unsuitable quarry, serious religious song can also provide us with an illustration. It is hard to deny, for example, that there are certain verses in the biblical psalms which carry traces of a similar attitude, e.g., 'O do well unto Thy servant: I have stuck unto Thy testimonies.'[1]

The classical biblical instance of an apparently clear-cut experimental approach to the efficacy of prayer is that of the contest between Elijah and the prophets of Baal. On this occasion Elijah proposed a definite experiment to decide between the reality and power of Yahweh and that of Baal. 'Call ye on the name of your god, and I will call on the name of the Lord: and the God that answereth by fire, let him be God.'[2] John Wisdom accepts this episode at its face value, but admits that such an unsophisticated experiment in prayer is no longer a serious option for the believer of today. He comments: '. . . in spite of the persistence of an experimental element in some theistic belief, it remains true that Elijah's method on Mount Carmel of settling the matter of what god or gods exist would be far less appropriate today than it was then.'[3] I. T. Ramsey, on the other hand, raises the question whether the issue ever was, strictly speaking, experimental. In a discussion of the matter he makes the following three points. First, no generalization was involved in the procedure. It was not intended as a verification of some general rule concerning God's behaviour and Elijah's behaviour and the connexion between them. Certainly Elijah had not, as it were, mastered the divine mechanism so as to enable him to predict

[1] Psalm 119.131.
[2] I Kings 18.24.
[3] 'Gods', in: John Wisdom, *Philosophy and Psychoanalysis*, Oxford 1952, p. 149.

how in certain specific circumstances it would regularly work. Second, although Elijah seemed to be putting God to the test in no uncertain manner, such a test would be so blatantly irreligious that 'the religious man will say that it is not an experimental issue, but that Elijah is only seeking God's answer in prayer. Elijah is not verifying deductions, he is yielding himself in prayer, and trusting God for some—no matter what—visible answer.' Third, Ramsey asks the question: 'Was it better that God, so to say, "obliged"?' 'I am bound to say,' he continues, 'quite honestly, and I hope I may say it without irreverence, that I doubt whether it was. Suppose God *always* obliged as he did that afternoon, what would be the result? God would become no more than (at best) a super-scientific invariant, from which any and every deduction could be certain to be verified. To put the point otherwise: when God obliged that day, he surely laid on Elijah a much greater necessity than ever before for Elijah to be theologically circumspect. In many ways Elijah, we might say, might have had his religion in the long run enriched, if God had not displayed himself so vigorously and so verifiably on that afternoon.'[4] He stresses the point concerning the enrichment of the believer's religious life with a reference to the case of Jeremiah: '. . . it was in failing to find anything resembling, let alone anything able to be misunderstood as resembling, verifiable deductions that Jeremiah's religion rose to new and distinctive heights.'[5]

Putting on one side the question whether Ramsey is not further idealizing a story which originally may have been about a piece of sympathetic rain-magic—'the pouring of water on the altar and the subsequent ritual prostration of Elijah (probably crouching in such a way as to represent a cloud) at the top of Carmel constitute an acted prayer for rain'[6]—we may ask what it was that prompted Elijah to trust God, what he trusted God for, and in what way his religion would have been 'enriched' if God's answer seldom or never matched his hopes and desires. In ordinary human

---

[4] Ian T. Ramsey, *Religion and Science: Conflict & Synthesis*, London 1964, p. 71.
[5] *Ibid*.
[6] J. Mauchline in Matthew Black and H. H. Rowley (eds.), *Peake's Commentary on the Bible*, London 1962, p. 346.

relationships we may go on trusting someone even though the evidence seems to suggest to the impartial observer that our trust is misplaced, but our original trust is not unrelated to the evidence we possess that the one we trust at least takes note of our own desires and needs and has our well-being at heart. We may say, then, that God surely knows our real needs better than we know them ourselves, and that we can trust him to do what is best even though it may appear to us otherwise, but we should have little reason for saying any such thing if we *never* discovered him meeting what we ourselves honestly and reflectively believe to be our needs. There is plenty of room for reverent agnosticism in our presenting our petitions before the throne of heaven, but there may come a point where agnosticism ceases to be reverent and an approach to heaven is conscientiously abandoned in favour of an unbelieving regulation of one's own affairs. If we are to have some good reason for trusting God, then we must have reason to believe that God is trustworthy. We must be prepared to give an answer to the question why we go on trusting God in circumstances in which such trust appears to the impartial observer to be misplaced. Our reasons will no doubt be highly complex; but we may surely expect that there will be something in our experience which 'verifies' our faith in his grace and favour. Furthermore, if we continue to make our petitions to him, we may expect to be able to point to some occasion or occasions on which we can properly claim that he has answered them. If there is nothing to be said in support of our belief, then the fitting conclusion seems to be that God, if there is a God, has no real concern for us and that therefore he is no concern of ours.

The problem of evidence is a pressing problem. Despite what we have said about the impropriety of a totally impersonal experimental approach to the problem on the grounds that personal elements are inevitably involved, might it not be possible, while granting the presence of these personal factors, to undertake some sort of statistical investigation? Might we not expect to find some significant variations in the course of events between those otherwise similar occasions on which prayer has been offered and those on which it has not? Such, at any rate, seems to have been the point

c

of view of Francis Galton, who, writing in 1883, set himself to answer 'the simple statistical question—Are prayers answered, or are they not?'[7] He left on one side any discussion of 'isolated and remarkable instances', and proposed 'to examine large classes of cases, and to be guided by broad averages'. He could find no evidence to suggest that sick persons who prayed, or who were prayed for, recovered on the average more rapidly than others, and he observed that he knew of no single instance 'in which papers read before statistical societies have recognized the agency of prayer either on disease or on anything else'. He added the comment that 'the universal habit of the scientific world to ignore the power of prayer is a very important fact'. Perhaps his most intriguing investigation concerned the longevity of 'persons whose lives are publicly prayed for', such as sovereigns, and of 'the praying classes generally', such as clergy. From statistics available for the years 1758 to 1843 he discovered that 'sovereigns are literally the shortest lived of all who have the advantage of affluence', and he concluded that the prayer, 'Grant her in health long to live', had no efficacy, 'unless the very questionable hypothesis be raised, that the conditions of royal life may naturally be yet more fatal, and that their influence is partly, though incompletely, neutralized by the effect of public prayers'. Again, an examination of the statistics comparing the longevity of clergy, lawyers and medical men led him to the conclusion that 'the prayers of the clergy for protection against the perils and dangers of the night, for security during the day, and for recovery from sickness, appear to be futile in result'. Straying beyond the purely statistical approach, he remarked that 'the procedure of convocation, which, like all exclusively clerical meetings, is opened with prayer, has not inspired the outer world with much respect', and he went on to castigate not only the practice of prayer, but also the belief in any sort of over-ruling providence. 'It was at one time considered an act of mistrust in an over-ruling Providence to put lightning conductors on churches; for it was said that God would surely take care of His own. But Arago's collection of the

[7] Sir Francis Galton, *Inquiries into the Human Faculty and its Development*, London 1883, p. 277.

accidents from lightning showed they were sorely needed; and now lightning conductors are universal.' The upshot of all this is a determined plea to be rid of the superstitious belief in the objective efficacy of prayer. 'The civilized world has already yielded an enormous amount of honest conviction to the inexorable requirements of solid fact; and it seems to me clear that all belief in the efficacy of prayer, in the sense in which I have been considering it, must be yielded also. The evidence I have been able to collect bears wholly and solely in that direction, and in the face of it the *onus probandi* must henceforth lie on the other side.'[8]

What are we to make of this? Are we to appeal to the 'evidence' of those who claim to have had answers to their prayers? That there are certain intangibles which do affect the course of illness, such as hope, or the will to live, many doctors would nowadays admit. Is prayer another of these intangibles? Is the action of God in answer to prayer such that it escapes the net of generalization and statistical formulation, but is operative nevertheless? Is it possible to isolate the element of prayer from all other relevant aspects of the total situation and so set up a properly controlled experiment in which the variation of other factors is immaterial to the results? Or are we taking a wrong turning in pursuing the language of request and answer in too close a dependence on the human analogy? Does the error lie in our asking God to 'do' things? Or, to put the question in a slightly different way, are the things which God 'does' in answer to our prayers of a different order from the things we do in the world in answer to the requests of our fellows?

If we must be careful of the dangers involved in making an objectively *experimental* issue out of prayer, lest we find ourselves deserting the insights of religion for the delusions of magic, may we perhaps claim that there is a discernible *experiential* side to prayer? 'Taste and see how gracious the Lord is.' Does the actual experience of praying provide the believer with all the evidence he needs? Even if the subjective experience of the man who prays

[8] An account of a recent attempt to undertake a statistical survey of the effects of intercession on the recovery of the sick may be found in the *Journal of Chronic Diseases*, 1965, Vol. 18, pp. 367-377: C. R. B. Joyce and R. M. C. Weldon, 'The Objective Efficacy of Prayer: a double-blind clinical trial.'

differs, as well it may, from that of the man who does not pray, we still have to ask how to interpret this experience. Is it simply an activity of the human consciousness which is its own answer, like singing to keep one's courage up? Or do we claim that there is also revealed to us an activity of God which is other than our own activity, and which, though moving secretly in the depths of our hearts and minds, is properly described as issuing in answer to our prayer? Can an appeal to experience get us any further than an appeal to experiment?

In the first volume of his Gifford Lectures, the distinguished zoologist, Sir Alister Hardy, argues that there is no alternative to our experimenting with prayer if it is to retain a permanent place in the life of modern man. He writes as follows: 'As our natural theology must be based upon a scientific approach so I believe our religion itself should be a dynamic faith—an experimental faith—a faith in the receiving of Grace in answer to prayer. Let us experiment and see. I don't mean selfish prayer for one's own safety or betterment or prayers to alter physical events, like praying for rain, but prayers to have help in our actions. Somehow, in some extraordinary way, I do believe that there is a vast store of wisdom and spiritual strength that we can tap in this way—something which is of the utmost importance to mankind.'[9] If there is indeed available to us such 'help in our actions', we must ask what sort of help this is. Is it in principle anything other than the help we might get for our writing from recollecting the advice, 'think before you ink'? Sir Alister, we may observe, uses both the personal language of help and answer, and also the impersonal language of tapping a store. These different analogies suggest different interpretations and, ultimately, different metaphysics. It is difficult to be sure what metaphysic the author has in mind, or whether he believes that the metaphysical issue is at all relevant. He quotes with approval Dr L. P. Jacks' words: 'There is that in the world, call it what you will, which responds to the confidence of those who trust it, declaring itself to them as a fellow-worker in the pursuit of the Eternal Values, meeting their loyalty to it with reciprocal loyalty to them. It

[9] Sir Alister Hardy, *The Living Stream*, London 1965, p. 285.

is a Power which can help, deliver, illuminate and gladden; the companion of the brave, the upholder of the loyal, the friend of the lover, the healer of the broken, the joy of the victorious—the God who is spirit, the God who is love.' Here again we notice the complete intermingling of personal and impersonal analogies, and we cannot but ask ourselves what is the ontological status of this Power which is itself 'a fellow-worker in the pursuit of the Eternal Values'.

Sir Alister adds this comment to Dr Jacks' words: 'At the *very least* I expect this power of which we speak may be some subconscious shared reservoir of spiritual "know-how" which we call Divine (perhaps something like the species "mind" that I have suggested). I think, however, it is *far more likely* that above this there is something much more wonderful to which we give the name God. But even if it *should* be shown, and I don't believe it will, that this whole conception is a purely psychological one and, if, in some way, this mind factor *should* eventually be proved to be entirely of physico-chemical origin—it would not to my mind destroy the joy or help of *the experience we may still call Divine* any more than it would destroy the glorious beauty felt in poetry or art.' We may agree that the quality of an experience is what it is, whatever the cause and origin of that experience. But to call an experience divine is more than to characterize its feeling-tone; it is to suggest that it has an over-all significance and to relate it in some fundamental and commanding way to the rest of our experiences, both in their subjective and their objective aspects. In fact these aspects cannot be completely separated. The joy and help which are associated with a particular experience are bound to vary according to the status and significance which we attribute to the content of that experience. For instance, there will very likely be a subtle difference of feeling, certainly a difference of consequential expectations, attitudes and behaviour-policies, between those who plot their religious experience solely within a psychological framework and those who also attribute to it revelatory significance about the character of what ultimately is the case about man, the world and God. Granted that we begin with our own experience, we soon find ourselves asking the question, what our experience is an experience *of*.

Do our experiences tell us only about ourselves, or do they also afford us some insight into what exists independently of ourselves? The word 'experience' is itself ambiguous in this respect. It is sometimes used so as to include both the subjective and the object- ive poles of our experience. At other times its meaning is restricted to the subjective pole. To treat divinity solely in psychological terms is to make a division between the subjective and the objective poles of experience and to exclude the latter as more or less irrelevant. The divine is seen as an aspect, albeit an important aspect, of human consciousness. The theological is reduced to the anthropological. Unless, however, we are prepared for such a radical redefinition of the concept of the divine, we must allow it, in some sense, an inclusiveness and comprehensiveness, an ultimacy which is prior to the division between the subjective and the objective and which is the ground of both. The divine encompasses *both* man *and* his world. In understanding and mastering his world man may stand back from it and distinguish himself from it. But the divine is not to be limited in this way to either side of the distinction. It tran- scends the distinction and provides a unity underlying the distinc- tion. It is the ground both of man's persistent desire to understand and of the concepts of his understanding. It supplies the bond be- tween subject and object. It is the unlimited presupposed by man's limited and limiting mode of discursive knowledge. Something like this, I suspect, is intended by Karl Jaspers when he writes: 'We are natures which not only inquire into the things in the world, but also into ourselves and into the Whole. Thus, to be sure, we are real only as empirical existents, as consciousness as such, and as spirit; but therein we are also beyond ourselves and beyond every determinate mode of our empirical existence, beyond any determinate content of thought, and in this "beyond" we first come to ourselves and to Transcendence.'[10] Or, again, when Ramsey speaks of a 'cosmic disclosure', I do not understand him to mean that our perceptual field is somehow enlarged to include, *per impossible*, the whole world, but that we are in some strange manner made aware of and

---

[10] Karl Jaspers, *Reason and Existence*, London 1956, pp. 110f.

enabled to acknowledge that which is both ultimate and all-inclusive. This would explain the way in which he is able to argue that there can be only one God, that it is logically absurd to talk about different Gods, however many different ideas of God we may have. 'If the word "God" had a completely adequate contextual setting it would be the name whose reference was the whole universe, and it is this, I believe, which justifies us meanwhile in claiming that the reference of any and every cosmic disclosure, i.e. a disclosure which is restricted to no finite pattern of spatio-temporal events as its centre, is the same, viz. God.'[11] God is that in which or through which or towards which all beings cohere, and in which they participate.

Having reviewed the possibility of an approach to the understanding of prayer by way of experiment and experience, we must now consider more closely this fundamental notion of participation as it reveals itself in the structure of man's religious experience and in his relationship to the Transcendent.

In his existence in the world a man is confronted on all sides by limitations. On the one hand there are the limitations of his own being, the gap disclosed between his promise and his performance, between what he has it in himself to be and what he actually succeeds in being, his being and his doing. On the other, there are the limitations of his world, consisting as it does of objects which are limited by one another, limited in space and time, limited in the fact that they are continually changing. Although he stands out from this world, although he can exercise a measure of freedom and responsibility over against it, he is nevertheless at the same time conscious that he is himself a part of this world. He himself is subject to chance and change, a product of nature. He is at home in nature, and yet he feels himself a pilgrim and sojourner. He appears to have a foot in two 'worlds', of nature and of spirit, and yet he believes the world is somehow one.

Now it may be argued that he is dimly aware, through all that changes, both within and without, of that which persists through change, which itself does not change. The best description of this awareness that I know is to be found in George Woods' essay on

[11] Ian T. Ramsey, *Christian Discourse*, London 1965, p. 82.

Transcendence in *Soundings*: 'In our own lives, we know the tremulous quality of our own existence. But do we have no sense of the unchanging beneath the changes which we see? Those who have lost effective belief in God continue to believe in Nature and the Natural Order which survives throughout all natural changes. There is here a belief in Nature as transcending all natural products. . . . If we come to think that Nature is itself a remoter process of change, we begin to think of some still more remote conditions of change which do not themselves change. We cannot rest in absolute change. In our experience of the changing, we have also a curious experience of the unchanging. I believe that we are gradually driven towards an awareness of some being, which is variously styled pure, absolute or transcendent. The conclusion is being itself.'[12] (In these days when we hear much of the necessity of abandoning the category of substance in favour of that of process, it is refreshing to hear a voice raising the question whether the concept of absolute change is not after all absolute nonsense, and whether we are not in some way aware of that which is as well as of that which becomes.)

The religious man, in recognizing the powers of transcendent being, acknowledges the fact that there is a bond between himself and the transcendent being which is the supporting ground of becoming. Whatever the true etymology of the word *religio*, it is not inappropriate to describe religion as 'bondage' to transcendent being, with the reminder that not all bonds are necessarily the bonds of slavery. There are also bonds of friendship, loyalty and love. It is possible, then, that there may also be a religious bondage which is not ineptly characterized as 'perfect freedom'.

While acknowledging this bond between himself and transcendent being, the religious man may interpret the nature of this bond in various ways and use different analogies in order to make it intelligible to himself. Nevertheless the bond itself, as he sees it, is as ultimate as the transcendent being which he acknowledges. He himself, as man, is dependent on this being. He may ignore the bond, and he is free to disown it, but he cannot be rid of it. There is no

---

[12] *Soundings*, ed. A. R. Vidler, Cambridge 1962, p. 63.

possibility of divorce. Just as he cannot help existing in the world and being a part of the world, so he cannot help existing in a binding relationship to this transcendent being. He can disregard it, but he cannot opt out of it.

The irreligious man, on the other hand, acknowledges no such bond. He may admit that there is in fact a more or less universal religious bondage, but he asserts that this is only a contingency of human history, and that in order to achieve his full humanity man may and must break this entailment from the past. It is his moral task *'religionum nodis animos exsolvere'* (Lucretius).[13] He suspects all talk of transcendence. For him 'Nature' does not significantly transcend, except by way of extrapolation, the regularities which are observable in the objective world. There is here no suggestion of a *metabasis eis allo genos*, a jump to another kind of being. The language of transcendence may find some application at the human level; but even here it refers only to the possibilities of man's making himself by his free decisions 'more' than he already is. There is no Humanity transcending and embracing individual human beings. All religion breaks on the anvil of man's freedom. It is his destiny to accomplish his own salvation.

Let us return to the language of religion. Religious insight expresses itself in a series of complementary opposites, varying according to the different images selected, but all in some way contrasting the limited and imperfect with the unlimited and perfect. We may speak of becoming and being, or of the natural and the supernatural, or of appearance and reality, or of the secular and the sacred, or of time and eternity, or of the present age and the age to come. The character of a man's religion is to be discerned in the way in which he recognizes, understands and seeks to reconcile these opposites, in the way in which he acknowledges and accepts his relationship to transcendent being. In the way in which he interprets and lives out this relationship he finds his salvation. In coming to God he comes to himself.

This fundamentally dialectical structure of religious experience is clearly and movingly illustrated in a poem of Bonhoeffer, whose

---

[13] To free men's minds from religion's bonds.

name, oddly enough, is more usually ascribed with 'religionless' Christianity. The title of the poem, 'Who am I?' reflects the older and more traditional form of the religious question, 'What must I do to be saved?':

> Who am I? They often tell me
> I would step from my cell's confinement
> calmly, cheerfully, firmly,
> like a squire from his country-house.
> Who am I? They often tell me
> I would talk to my warders
> freely and friendly and clearly,
> as though it were mine to command.
>
> Who am I? They also tell me
> I would bear the days of misfortune
> equably, smilingly, proudly,
> like one accustomed to win.
>
> Am I then really all that which other men tell of?
> Or am I only what I know of myself,
> restless and longing and sick, like a bird in a cage,
> struggling for breath, as though hands were compressing my throat,
> yearning for colours, for flowers, for the voices of birds,
> thirsting for words of kindness, for neighbourliness,
> tossing in expectation of great events,
> powerlessly trembling for friends at an infinite distance,
> weary and empty at praying, at thinking, at making,
> faint, and ready to say farewell to it all?
>
> Who am I? This or the other?
> Am I one person today and tomorrow another?
> Am I both at once? A hypocrite before others,
> and before myself a contemptibly woebegone weakling?
> Or is something within me still like a beaten army,
> fleeing in disorder from victory already achieved?
>
> Who am I? They mock me, these lonely questions of mine.
> Whoever I am, thou knowest, O God, I am thine![14]

In the final line of this poem we have, expressed in the form of prayer, a religious affirmation which answers, without silencing,

[14] Dietrich Bonhoeffer, *Letters and Papers from Prison*, rev. ed., London 1967, pp. 197f.

the host of preceding questions which press towards the real being of a man's existence in the world. The remorseless interrogation of an individual's own being by the contradictions of his experience is met by the acknowledgment of the being of God as the ultimate being to whom he himself belongs.

The religious man, then, seeks the firm centre and completion of his own being in relationship to transcendent being. The character which he ascribes to this relationship and the manner in which he seeks to realize it vary from person to person and from religion to religion. Because of his sense of belonging, of participating in this transcendent being, of deriving his own being from it, he may perhaps fasten upon the analogy of a relationship between part and whole, and develop the idea of a Whole which somehow includes both himself and his world, thus embracing and comprehending both subjective and objective poles of his experience.

For example, he may think of Nature as an *organic* unity, its life flowing through his own being and that of the world around him. His religion, then, becomes a communion with Nature, a search for that vital unity which underlies the separation between the subjective and the objective.

Such religion can be illustrated from the writings of numerous nature 'mystics',[15] such as the nineteenth-century Richard Jefferies. It can take various forms and expresses itself in various ways. Wordsworth may or may not be properly included in such company. Zaehner, for example, doubts whether he had any 'intuitive realization of the identity or union of the individual with something else, either with Nature, or with God, or with that unidentifiable entity which Huxley calls the "Not-self" and which may be distinct from both'. Religious experience of this type is frequently interpreted in an anti-rational, anti-moral, and anti-personal way. Man's rational and moral endeavours are seen as destructive of his true religious being. A striking and recent example of such an outlook is to be found in Pär Lagerkvist's novel, *Pilgrim at Sea*. The unfrocked priest speaks of the sea as 'holy' and 'indifferent', holy because of its all-encompassing indifference:

[15] See especially R. C. Zaehner, *Mysticism Sacred and Profane*, Oxford 1957, Ch. III.

How should one grasp anything of life—understand and penetrate men and their ideas—until one has learnt from the sea? How should one see through their empty strivings and odd ambitions until one has looked out over the sea, which is boundless and sufficient in itself? Until one has learnt to think like the sea and not like these restless creatures who fancy that they're going somewhere, and that this going is the most important thing of all—that the goal is the meaning and purpose of their life? Until one has learnt to be carried along by the sea, to surrender to it utterly, and cease fretting about right and wrong, sin and guilt, truth and falsehood, god and evil—about salvation and grace and eternal damnation—about devil and god and their childish disputes? Until one has become as indifferent and free as the sea and will let oneself be carried, aimless, out into the unknown—surrender utterly to the unknown—to uncertainty as the only certainty, the only really dependable thing when all's said and done? Until one has learnt all that?[16]

Here the 'benign indifference of the universe', to use Camus's phrase,[17] is interpreted as an invitation to religious communion, where others might see it as a reason for the total rejection of religion and for the assertion of human freedom and responsibility in a world in which man finds himself a stranger.

Alternatively, the religious man may think of Nature as a *rational* unity, its necessary and universal reason embracing and reflected in his own rationality. His religion, then, becomes a search for that necessity of pattern which structures his own being and the being of the world, and a recognition of the fact that, whether he discovers it or not, such a structure must exist. All things are what they are because they could not conceivably be otherwise. They are ordered rationally and ordered well. Whatever happens happens necessarily and for the best possible reason.

Stoicism provides one obvious example of this kind of interpretation of the religious relationship. The Stoic doctrine of providence asserts that everything occurs in accordance with the divine reason. The proper religious response, therefore, is one of rational conformity. What appear to us to be evils would, if we could see the complete pattern, no longer appear as evil. No man can do anything in the long run but comply with this universal scheme of things. The

---

[16] Pär Lagerkvist, *Pilgrim at Sea*, London 1964, p. 12.
[17] Albert Camus, *The Outsider* (Penguin Books edition), p. 120.

truly religious man, the truly rational man, complies voluntarily
and whole-heartedly. So Cleanthes can pray:

> Lead me, O Zeus, and lead me, Destiny,
> Whither ordained is by your decree.
> I'll follow, doubting not, or if with will
> Recreant I falter—I shall follow still.[18]

In the same vein, Epictetus epitomizes the Stoic doctrine of providence when he writes: 'We ought to approach God as we approach
a guide, dealing with him as we deal with our eyes, not beseeching
him to show us one sort of thing rather than another, but accepting
the impressions of things as they are shown us. But instead of that,
we tremble and get hold of the augur and appeal to him as if he
were a god, and say, "Master, have pity, suffer me to come off
safe". Slave! Do you not wish for what is better for you? Is anything better than what seems good to God?[19] God's providence is
to be found not in his providing this *rather than* that, but in his
providing this *and* that. Acceptance of this providential ordering of
nature brings man to his true being, and gives him peace and freedom. 'Man, be bold at last—even to despair, as the phrase is—that
you may have peace and freedom and a lofty mind. Lift up your
neck at last, as one released from slavery. Have courage to look up
to God and say, "Deal with me hereafter as Thou wilt: I am as one
with Thee. I am Thine: I flinch from nothing, so long as Thou
thinkest it good. Lead me where Thou wilt. Put on me what
raiment Thou wilt. Wouldest Thou have me hold office, or
eschew it, stay or fly, be poor or rich? For all this I will defend
Thee before men. I will show each thing in its true nature, as it
is." '[20]

At the root of this acceptance of providence is the conviction that
what is, is good. The rational structure of things is teleological, *sub
specie boni*. Reason and goodness are two sides of one and the same
coin. Acceptance of the will of God is also love of God. We may

---

[18] Prayer, cited by Epictetus, *Enchiridion*, 53, trans. P. E. Matheson, *Epictetus, the
Discourses, and Manual*, London 1916.

[19] Epictetus, *Discourses*, II, vii, 11f., quoted in *Later Greek Religion*, ed. E. Bevan,
London 1927, p. 110.

[20] Epictetus, *Discourses*, II, xvi, 41f., Bevan, p. 111.

recall here Spinoza's expression of the joy and blessedness inherent in *'mentis acquiescentia'*, as well as his description of the intellectual love of God: 'The intellectual love of the mind towards God is the very love with which he loves himself, not in so far as he is infinite, but in so far as he can be manifested through the essence of the human mind, considered under the form of eternity; that is to say, the intellectual love of the mind towards God is part of the infinite love with which God loves himself.'[21] The precise significance of these words is notoriously difficult to grasp, but we may say at least that Spinoza is here using the language of part and whole to express the religious relationship in which he believes man stands to his necessarily existing God. The question remains whether this language of part and whole can do justice either to the freedom and personal responsibility of man or to the evil which at least appears to characterize parts of the whole when judged from the here and now. With regard to the latter question, for example, can concentration on the character of the Whole, rather than on that of the parts which go to make up the Whole, whether in terms of logical necessity or of aesthetic balance, really reconcile us to the manifest defects of some of the parts?

Because of these manifest defects in the world others have sought the completion of their own being, not in dependence on the world, whether interpreted as an organic or a rational whole, but in communion with that which is other than the world. Transcendent being is to be found, not in and through the world, but only in contrast to the world. At the best the world is a pale reflection of this being, at the worst it is illusion. Hence the religious man turns away from the world and seeks his salvation in a relationship with a transcendent being which he interprets as world-rejecting. There is no rhyme or reason in the world. The soul must press beyond the world if it is to discover its own true being.

Within this over-all context, religious experience and its interpretation may develop in different ways. Those who set store by the rationality of man may interpret the religious relationship as a communion between man's rational soul and a world of ideal form,

[21] Spinoza, *Ethics*, Book V, Prop. 36.

culminating in an intuitive vision of the Good which is the locus of all being and intelligibility. The soul seeks by a rational ascesis to be liberated from the world of appearance, the world of the senses, and to return to the world of ideal reality. It is itself already akin to this ideal world. It is drawn back towards this ideal world by a movement of intellectual desire. Man's rationality is itself religious in that it binds man to this ideal world. The movement of thought is a movement towards the Good, it is an assimilation to deity. There is no room here for a dialogue of prayer in any personal sense, but there is a movement of the mind towards that ultimate reality from which the reality of man's own being derives. The Good does not move towards man, but it attracts man towards itself.

A rational religion of this Platonic type has proved not unattractive to Christian thought. It is questionable, however, whether it is really compatible with Christian theism. If we want to see the radical ambiguity for religion inherent in a view which emphasizes the rationality and moral freedom of man, we can find a clear illustration in the thought of Kant. On the one hand it is man's rational freedom which gives him access to the noumenal world, to what is in itself, whatever the appearances of the phenomenal world may be. The moral law is at one and the same time the law of man's own being and an expression of transcendent being. Consequently it evokes a religious response and man very properly feels a reverence towards it. On the other hand, when Kant comes to discuss the practice of religion, although he does his best to make room for the workings of divine grace, he cannot bring himself to allow that man may rightly pray for grace. Man may receive grace; but he has to earn it. And whether he receives it or not is in no way dependent upon his praying for it. Kant speaks of 'the illusion of being able to bring about, through the use of merely natural means, an effect which is, for us, a mystery, namely, the influence of God upon our morality'.[22] Praying, then, belongs to the natural, phenomenal world. Free obedience to the moral law provides the sole and

---

[22] Immanuel Kant, *Religion Within the Limits of Reason Alone*, New York 1956, p. 182.

adequate bond between man and the noumenal world.[23] The only prayer which Kant fully countenances is the prayer which is 'a heartfelt wish to be well-pleasing to God in our every act and abstention, or in other.words, the disposition, accompanying all our actions, to perform these as though they were being executed in the service of God'.[24] This kind of prayer, he adds, can be prayed 'with perfect sincerity' even by the man who 'does not presume to be able to affirm that the existence of God is wholly certain', because it 'arises in the moral disposition (animated solely by the idea of God), and, as the moral spirit of prayer, brings about its object (being well pleasing to God) of itself. Only such a prayer can be prayed with *faith*, and by this faith we mean the assurance that the prayer will *be heard*.'[25] The prayer is 'heard' precisely because there is no need for it to be heard. A man answers his own prayer—for a right moral disposition—in the very act of praying.

Others, again, have sought communion with the transcendent by overcoming the separation between the self and the transcendent and by merging the self in God. In this kind of religious experience the soul is isolated from everything else and seeks a state of being in which all distinctions are overcome and in which God and the self are one and the same. Mystical monism of this kind branches out into a variety of forms which I have neither the time nor the knowledge to explore. I mention this type of religion here only to draw attention to the recurring pattern of man's sense of participation in that which transcends the limitations both of himself and of his world. It is communion with transcendent being which offers a man salvation.

It is high time to bring these sketchy observations to an end. In our attempt to elucidate the nature and function of prayer and its relation to divine providence we began by considering the possibility of an appeal to experiment and experience. The difficulties which we encountered here led us to examine the fundamental structure of religion. We argued that at the heart of religion there is to be

[23] We may in passing compare Seneca's remark: 'How foolish to pray for a good spirit, since you can win that for yourself.'

[24] *Op. cit.*, p. 183.

[25] *Op. cit.*, pp. 183f.

found the acknowledgment of transcendent being, of that which ultimately is, of God. The being of God is both ultimate and unlimited. That is, there is no going beyond it to something yet more ultimate, nor is it subject to the limitations which characterize finite beings. The character of God's being and of man's relationship to it may be interpreted in a variety of different ways. These different interpretations give shape to the different forms which religion can develop. Nevertheless, the conviction that the fulfilment of man's own being is bound up with his achieving a right relationship with this transcendent being is common to all such interpretations. Man is essentially dependent on transcendent being, and the acceptance of this dependence is the religious attitude *par excellence*. It may be described as self-surrender, self-sacrifice, or self-noughting. But however it is described, it is basically the acknowledgment that we have not made ourselves and cannot make ourselves, but that we receive our true being from God. Whatever happens to us, whatever we ourselves do or desire, God Is. It is for us to acknowledge his being and to accept our dependence. Herein lies our salvation. This being the case, prayer can now be seen for what it essentially is. It stems from the expression and cultivation of this attitude of dependence. It is the conscious surrender of ourselves to God, come what may.

At this point two questions force themselves upon our attention. The first has already briefly attracted our notice. It stems from our own character as free moral beings, involved in the conflict between good and evil, in the ceaseless struggle to promote the good. Have we adequate *moral* grounds for adopting a religious attitude? What is this ultimate reality which claims our surrender? Has it any rightful claim upon our acceptance? Why *should* we surrender ourselves? The Book of Job is a profoundly religious book, and the man who has not wrestled with the problems of Job has not wrestled with the realities of religion. But did Job do well to acknowledge his own nonentity when finally he was confronted with the overwhelming power and impenetrable mystery of God?

The second question stems from the character of Christian faith. If religion is the response to that which ultimately is, whatever may

D

come to pass in the world, what are we to make of the Christian gospel which proclaims not only that God is creator of all things visible and invisible, but also that at a particular time and in a particular place 'the Word was made flesh'? What has happened here to the transcendence and universality of God?

Bringing the two questions together we may ask whether the religious answer of the book of Job satisfies either our moral or our Christian convictions.

III

Mystery and Presence

W E have been arguing that at the heart of religious experience there lies a double sense, on the one hand of human limitation and imperfection and on the other of the Unlimited and Perfect to which man properly belongs and in which he somehow participates. The religious man is conscious of a paradox within his own being. He is in the world but not of the world. This experience often finds expression in a series of complementary opposites—the changing and the unchanging, the finite and the infinite, the temporal and the eternal—and religions may be classified according to the way in which these apparent opposites are thought to be related to each other. The limited creature, man, by virtue of his humanity already participates in the Unlimited, but he has still to discover and realize the proper manner of this participation. He has to become what he really is. This is the religious quest. He remains a stranger to his own true being in so far as he fails to realize his proper relationship to this perfect Being. A metaphysical urge prompts him to press beyond the limits of his discursive understanding of the finite world, to discover a single system in which both finite and infinite may rationally be comprehended. A religious urge prompts him to seek salvation through communion with that which transcends his world and his understanding of it, and which remains essentially mysterious.

The religious man, then, has a sense of being in communion with that which transcends the intelligible world of finite objects, with that which ultimately is, whatever may or may not happen in the changing world of nature and history. Furthermore, the basic religious attitude is one of dependence and acceptance. As such it calls for self-surrender, or self-sacrifice. Prayer is the expression and cultivation of this attitude. The religious man surrenders himself and all that he is to God, come what may. He accepts, because he belongs to God, and God is ultimate and eternal. 'It is he that hath made us, and not we ourselves; we are his people, and the sheep of his pasture.'[1] The tone of this basic religious attitude is nowhere better expressed than by Schleiermacher, whatever we may think of his attempt to describe it in terms of immediate feeling, when he wrote: 'The contemplation of the pious is the immediate consciousness of the universal existence of all finite things, in and through the Infinite, and of all temporal things in and through the Eternal. . . . Where this is found religion is satisfied, where it hides itself there is for her unrest and anguish, extremity and death. . . . *Piety appears as a surrender, a submission to be moved by the Whole that stands over against men.*'[2] Whatever Schleiermacher may say elsewhere, the words which I have italicized seem to me to offer us a succinct expression both of the ultimacy and transcendence of God and also of the religious attitude of self-surrender about which we have been talking.

An unrepentant emphasis on the transcendence of God is fundamental to a proper interpretation of religion, but it raises sharply some very difficult questions. The recognition that we are at all points surrounded by ultimate Mystery may be the beginning of religion, but the notion itself is strangely puzzling.

First, then, we must raise the question whether the idea of God is anything more than a negative idea, the idea of something we know not what. Is it possible to give any positive content to the idea of ultimate and transcendent being? Do we not arrive at this idea by a *via negativa*, the merest suggestion of a being which is other than finite being and which is not restricted by the limitations of finite being? We are conscious of certain ever-changing boundaries

[1] Psalm 100.3.
[2] F. Schleiermacher, *On Religion. Speeches to its Cultured Despisers*, New York 1958, pp. 36f.

of our experience, and these boundaries may suggest the possibility of a Beyond which is itself unbounded; but have we here anything more concrete than a Kantian idea of reason, a kind of 'limiting' concept which is itself unlimited? For example, the exclamation 'God alone knows' may be merely an indication of our human ignorance rather than a positive affirmation of divine omniscience. Or are we in some manner or other directly aware of this Beyond, with a kind of immediate apprehension which Kant himself did not recognize? That is, are there instances in which we apprehend the reality of this transcendent being, and do not simply propose to ourselves its ideal possibility? Let us suppose that it is a fact that we are sometimes conscious of apprehending it, or at least of being apprehended by it. Can we say anything positive about it, or does it not remain utterly mysterious? If it makes no discernible difference to the world in which we live and we are unable to grasp it by the concepts of our empirical understanding, does it not remain in a very real sense unknowable? And if unknowable, then, practically speaking, irrelevant? It may in some odd way provide a mysterious metaphysical foundation for the world of our ordinary experience, but why should it present itself to us religiously as a *mysterium tremendum et fascinans*, or as an object of our ultimate concern?

This brings us to our second question. Granted that we are sometimes aware of such transcendent being, of that which encompasses our world and ourselves, what is there about it which would justify our surrendering and submitting ourselves to it and our allowing ourselves to be moved by it? Such a response may indeed be presented as a way of salvation, of solving the problem inherent in being a finite human self, but it may equally well be presented as a way of passivity, of flight from the realities of personal being and so of death to the human self. It is to be noted that Schleiermacher himself made a clear-cut distinction between piety and morality, and we shall be considering in more detail in the next lecture the full force of morality's protest against the religious attitude. But here we may to a degree anticipate our later discussion, and in the present context of the mysterious transcendence of God raise the general question why we should surrender ourselves to this transcendent being if we know nothing about it except the fact of its transcendence. Is this mysterious being really gracious towards our own moral, personal and spiritual being? Does it really merit our self-surrender? Does it call forth our worship and adoration? Outside an American church there was once, I am told, the notice: 'God loves each one of you; so does your Rector.' Now there is nothing in principle to prevent our observing the Rector's behaviour in order to verify the assertion concerning his love for each of his parishioners. If he did in fact love them, we should expect to find him doing certain things and not doing certain things, behaving in this way rather than in that way. But what of the love of God, whose being and activity transcends the distinctions of the finite world, and who is said to love, *whatever* happens? In a word, are we justified in saying that God is good?

It may be argued in traditional terms that the perfection of God entails his goodness, that he is good simply because his being is without limitation. The implied notion that all evil is somehow a limitation, a defect of being, is one which I find difficult to understand and to which I could certainly not do justice here. Let me content myself with the comment that this is not obviously the case. What is is not self-evidently good in so far as it is. Certainly in the way in which we ordinarily speak of perfection, we distinguish between evaluative and descriptive concepts of perfection. We can speak of a perfect circle, or a perfect square. We can even speak of a perfect murder. In none of these cases are we expressing our moral approval. Now in so far as we arrive at a concept of the perfection of God by contrasting the notion of perfect being with that of finite being we do not obviously bring in ideas of moral perfection. Indeed it is more tempting to say that God transcends even the distinction between good and evil, and that he embraces both.

It may, again, be argued that the affirmation that God is good is in no way comparable to the affirmation that a human person is good. Rather it is to be understood in terms of an act of self-surrender. Its use is performatory rather than evaluative or descriptive. When we say that God is good, we are not making an assertion about God so much as expressing and realizing our own acceptance. It is something like the exclamation 'Well and good!', which does little more than embody our bare assent. But whereas we usually give voice to an exclamation such as this with reference to some particular state of affairs which might have been otherwise, the affirmation that God is good expresses our acceptance of that which underlies and makes possible any and every state of affairs, of the ultimate fact that there is a state of affairs, and it is frequently made in a context in which the particular state of affairs concerned is far from good in the straightforward sense of the word. The same kind of ultimate acceptance is to be found in the language of the Psalmist: 'Thou art he that took me out of the womb; thou didst make me trust when I was upon my mother's breasts. I was cast upon thee from the womb: thou art my God from my mother's belly.'[3] At this point, however, we come back again to the question which we raised earlier, whether religious self-surrender may not be a way of death, a reversion to an all-embracing pre-natal existence when the self no longer stands apart from its world and often in uneasy tension with it, but is again at one with its world as before birth the unborn infant was one with its mother. If the affirmation that God is good is an expression of self-surrender of this kind and nothing more, then the derivative notion of the goodness of God is thoroughly equivocal. It does not bear even an analogical relationship to the notion of the goodness of man, since it does not refer to any identifiable characteristic of God at all. It appears to refer to the character of God, but in fact it merely expresses the self-surrender of man. It is difficult to distinguish it from the equally self-surrendering exclamation, 'I give up!' It is just this equivocality which evokes a protest in the name of goodness itself. The best-known protest is probably that of J. S. Mill: 'I will call no being good who is not what I mean when I apply that epithet to my fellow creatures, and if such a being can sentence me to hell for not so calling him, to hell I will go.' We call our fellow-creatures good because they possess certain characteristics and lack others. Now it may be legitimate

---

[3] Psalm 22.9f.

and necessary to speak analogically when we ascribe goodness to God. Here, however, it seems that we are being invited to call God good simply because he is what he is, ultimate but utterly mysterious.

When Job answered the Lord, who had spoken to him out of the whirlwind about the foundations of the earth, about the Pleiades and the Mazzaroth, about behemoth and leviathan, with the words: 'I know that thou canst do all things, and that no purpose of thine can be restrained. . . . Wherefore I abhor myself, and repent in dust and ashes',[4] he certainly gave voice to one important aspect of the truth with which any adequate exposition of religious belief has to deal, namely, the hiddenness of God and our own inability fully to comprehend his ways. Even so it seems to me that here we are not altogether free of what I may venture to call the 'headmaster' approach to religion. 'Who are you, boy, to dare to question my authority and wisdom?!' Authority becomes another name for power. If authority must never be questioned, or if it consistently refuses to reveal the grounds of its own claims, it all too easily degenerates into the exercise of naked power. We do well to be cautious in any claim we may make to understand the ways of God, but an allegiance based on total incomprehension has little to be said in its favour! The earlier celebrated affirmation of Job, 'Though he slay me, yet will I trust in him',[5] breathes a very different atmosphere. Job is surely expressing here a deep conviction that God will *not* ultimately and finally slay him. Beyond the worst that can happen to him in this life he still dares to hope, because he believes God to be trustworthy. His confession of faith is both performatory and assertive. It expresses both commitment and belief. It is an act of self-surrender and a statement about the character of God.

Leaving on one side the whole tangle of logical difficulties involved in the claim that the affirmation that God is good is at least in part an assertion about God, in particular the difficulties concerning its verification, we may simply make the point that the affirmation that God is good implicitly includes an affirmation that the attributes of God justify our confession of faith. Such faith, it is claimed, is, humanly speaking, appropriate. There is a real analogy

---

[4] Job 42.2, 6.   [5] Job 13.15. The reading is uncertain.

between the goodness of God and what is good for man. The religious act of self-surrender is an act which fulfils the values which are proper to man. He that loses his life for God's sake finds it.

However strongly we may wish to stress the mystery and transcendence of God, we must insist just as strongly that, if we are to give a reason for commending the religious attitude of acceptance and self-surrender, we must be able to make some positive assertions about the attributes of God. We must be able in some way to penetrate the veil of mystery. God must present himself to us in his self-commending goodness. Now the Christian gospel proclaims that God has done just this. He has revealed himself for what, in his ultimate transcendence, he eternally is. We turn, then, to consider the nature of this gospel, and in particular the light which it claims to shed on the mystery of the divine being.

Emphasis on the transcendence of God makes him remote from us. He is no longer part and parcel of the empirical world in which we live. He is no longer subject to the limitations which determine beings which have their existence in the world. He embraces them. He is the God of nature, not a natural god. He is the Lord of history, not an historical lord. There are gods many and lords many, but only One who is.

Thus the journey along the *via negativa* removes more and more features from the face of God until he threatens to become completely mysterious and utterly transcendent. There is little left save the suspicion of a smile. The Christian gospel, however, proclaims that at a certain time and in a certain place, amid all the concrete particularities of history, the transcendent God revealed himself. 'The Word became flesh, and dwelt among us (and we beheld his glory, glory as of the only begotten from the Father), full of grace and truth.'[6] On a wider canvas we find that the scriptures are full of references to the purposes of God and of his activity in the affairs of men. He speaks to men, not only in the picturesque way in which it is recounted that he held converse with Adam and Eve in the garden of Eden, but also in the more sophisticated way in which he utters his word to the prophets. His word is also his action. He

[6] John 1.14.

makes a covenant through Moses with the people of Israel. He calls and he sends, he commands and he promises, he acts and he refrains from acting. There is nothing purely universal about such activity; it is also highly selective and particular. 'You only have I known of all the families of the earth.'[7] Thus we are given a portrayal of a God who acts, of a living God who is intimately involved in all that is going on in the world, who himself participates with man in the course of history. Moreover, it is to this God that prayer is made. Frequently it takes the form of direct petition, uttered in the confident hope that God will hear and answer if the petition accords with his own will. Sometimes a man will plead with God, as he might with a fellow man. For example, Abraham pleads with the Lord on behalf of Sodom. 'Peradventure there be fifty righteous within the city.'[8] Or forty-five. Or forty, or thirty-five, or twenty, or even ten. And with great patience and forbearance the Lord promises to spare Sodom for the sake of the ten righteous inhabitants. This element of pleading is still to be found in the New Testament. The disciple is to be importunate in his prayers. He is to make his requests known to God. 'Ask, and it shall be given you; seek, and ye shall find; knock and it shall be opened unto you.'[9] 'If ye, then, being evil, know how to give good gifts unto your children, how much more shall your Father which is in heaven give good things to them that ask him?'[10]

This notion of asking God suggests that God may act in some specific way in answer to man's prayer, and that this activity, consequent upon man's request, may cause something to happen in the world which might otherwise not have happened. Now it is obvious that there are important distinctions to be made between making a request to a human being—or even to a super-human being—and making a request to God. For example, God *always* hears a man's prayer whether he answers it or not, whereas a Baal may sometimes be asleep or having a day off duty.[11] Or, again, God's will can *never* be bent to suit man's pleasure, whereas a human will all too frequently can. God remains God, and man man. Never-

[7] Amos 3.2.
[8] Genesis 18.24.
[9] Matthew 7.7.
[10] Matthew 7.11.
[11] See I Kings 18.

theless, when due allowance has been made for the difference between Creator and creature, there remains as a constant feature of biblical religion the conviction that God may answer a prayer by causing something specific to happen, or by refusing to cause something to happen. So David fasted and wept for Bathsheba's child while it was still alive, but when he heard that it had died he 'arose from the earth, and washed, and anointed himself, and changed his apparel; and he came into the house of the Lord, and worshipped: then he came to his own house; and when he required they set bread before him, and he did eat'. When his servants were astonished at this sudden change of behaviour, David answered: 'While the child was yet alive, I fasted and wept: for I said, who knoweth whether the Lord will not be gracious to me, that the child may live? But now he is dead, wherefore should I fast? Can I bring him back again? I shall go to him, but he shall not return to me.'[12] Death, we note, marks the point of no return. It is a boundary beyond which God's saving activity does not extend. There is a limit, then, to what one may properly ask of God; but until this limit is reached, the religious man continues to pray in hope.

What are we to think of these starkly anthropomorphic conceptions of God and prayer? In view of what we have been saying about the transcendence of God, we cannot but be ill at ease with them. But should we be right to reject them out of hand?

In his classic, *Prayer*, Friedrich Heiler defined the essential presuppositions of simple, unreflective prayer as follows: 'faith in the anthropomorphic character of God, in His real presence, in His changeability, in the reality of personal communion with Him.'[13] Heiler was himself convinced that philosophical reflection destroyed these essential presuppositions, and he ended his study of the history and psychology of prayer by presenting his readers with the necessity of making a choice between philosophy and prayer. 'There are only two possibilities,' he wrote; 'either decisively to affirm prayer "in its entirely non-rational character and with all its difficulties",

---

[12] II Samuel 12.20, 22f.
[13] F. Heiler, *Prayer: A Study in the History and Psychology of Religion*, Oxford 1932, p. 98.

as Ménégoz says, or to surrender genuine prayer and substitute for it adoration and devotion which resemble prayer. Every attempt to mingle the two conceptions violates psychological veracity.' If such is in fact our dilemma, it is an extremely painful one. Is it possible to make a rational choice between 'the entirely non-rational' and the rational without opting for the rational? One can certainly find room for the non-rational in life, but when it conflicts with what we believe to be rational, it is no longer non-rational, it is irrational. It seems, then, as if Heiler is confronting us with a choice between the rational and the irrational, between that which makes sense and that which makes nonsense. This is no real choice at all.

Be this as it may, Heiler's four presuppositions are not unlike those which underlie the biblical concepts of God and prayer. The biblical concept of God is certainly anthropomorphic in so far as it is personal rather than impersonal. The ultimate source and explanation of all things is traced back to the mind and will of God, to his wisdom and purpose, and not to some impersonal necessity of law or chance. It is true that such anthropomorphism is counterbalanced by a complementary insistence that God's thoughts are not as man's thoughts and that God's ways are not as man's ways. Such reverent agnosticism, however, does not extend so far as to questioning the propriety of using the anthropomorphic categories of personality in the first place. God's 'name' is 'I am'; his 'label' is not 'It is'.

Again, God is 'really present' in the world. He is admittedly not a part of the world, and it might be more accurate to speak of his presence *to* the world than his presence *in* the world. Nevertheless, the world is the object of his continuing care and concern, and the affairs of man and nations are under his providence and control. To those who have ears to hear and eyes to see are given signs of his present and continuing activity. A hidden God he may be, an absent God never.

Again, there can be no doubt, with regard to the biblical tradition, concerning the reality of personal communion with God. In the Old Testament there are those who have 'stood in the council of the Lord'[14] to perceive and hear his word. Moses himself 'the Lord

[14] Jeremiah 23.18.

knew face to face'.[15] While in the New Testament believers are brought into the presence of the Father through the work of the Son and in the power of the Holy Spirit. They enjoy the status of adoptive sonship. In the words of the Fourth Gospel, 'If a man love me, he will keep my word: and my Father will love him, and we will come unto him, and make our abode with him.'[16]

When we come to the changeability of God we find that we must discriminate between, on the one hand, the faithfulness of God, that is, his dependability, and on the other, his accommodation to the changing purposes of men. With God there can be 'no variation, neither shadow that is cast by turning'.[17] That is, his own being is eternal and unchanging. He cannot but be what he is. Likewise, his will and purposes are unchanging. They express his eternal being. Nevertheless, in pursuing this ultimate purpose he takes note of man's response or failure to respond. He is in dialogue with man. And if the dialogue is in any sense genuine and the encounter real, it seems that he must wait upon human response and in some relative but real sense be dependent on it.

The fundamental issue which lies behind the question of the changeability of God is that of the appropriateness of using personal analogies in describing the divine being and activity. The use of personal categories—categories of freedom, will, purpose, love, care, concern and the like—seems to be tied in a special way to notions of particularity and even of limitation. To be a person, in the ordinary sense of the word, is to be limited not only by the world but also by other persons. In fact human personality, though transcending the objective world, requires for its very existence an environment both of objects and of other persons. It would appear, then, that the application of personal categories to the transcendent God is doomed from the outset. This would certainly be the case if we interpreted these categories literally. There would be an unresolved opposition between universality and particularity, the unlimited and the limited. However, the literal application of any positive categories to God is similarly ruled out. Unless we are to rest content with the *via negativa*, ending in utter mystery, we shall be compelled to use

[15] Deuteronomy 34.10.　　[16] John 14.23.　　[17] James 1.17.

whatever analogies appear to us to be most like the truth. Certainly, 'all things end in mystery'. But if awareness of the mystery is especially associated with certain areas of our ordinary experience, these contexts may perhaps be allowed to supply the language in which we can give some positive account of the mystery. Let us then look more closely at this anthropomorphic language about God's activity in the world. What sense can we make of it without eroding its meaning completely?

Let us begin by looking at certain features of the use of personal language at the human level. When we speak of John's doings, we can at least identify John, either indirectly or by pointing him out. We can distinguish John's behaviour from Peter's behaviour. 'Look,' we may say, 'how shockingly John is behaving compared with Peter.' But what are we referring to when we speak of God's doings? Can we point to certain occurrences in the world and say that these are instances of God's activity—contrasted with other occurrences which are not also instances of God's activity?

It was once thought that we could do just this in the case of miracles. Miracles were identifiable examples of God's activity. Whereas in the ordinary run of events God's creative activity worked concurrently with the activity of secondary causes, in miraculous events there were no secondary causes and the miracle was directly caused by God himself. This belief, however, is open to serious objections. Can we be sure that we know the limits of the natural world and of the realm in which secondary causes operate? Again, even if we had good reason to believe that the unusual occurrence was not the product of any secondary cause, could we infer that it was therefore the product of a super-natural cause, that is, of God? Might it not have been an unpredictable, uncaused, rogue occurrence? These objections, perhaps, are not all equally insuperable. But there is a further objection which, from our immediate point of view, is more critical. If we wish to point to miraculous events in order to identify the activity of God, we are implying that he is active in the extraordinary events, p, q, r, but *not* in the ordinary events, x, y, z. We have thereby identified God at the expense of robbing him of his ultimacy and universality, and we have landed ourselves with a finite god of the gaps. It is useless to go on to say that he is also the cause of all other events, for by doing so we render invalid our attempt to identify his activity by response to a particular group of events.

Reference to God must be given in the first place by something like Ramsey's 'cosmic disclosure'. Only when we have indicated his universal activity may it be possible to go on to speak, in a certain sense, of his particular activity. Or to put the same point in another way. If we wish to describe some particular complex of finite events as the activity of *God*, we must already have arrived at our concept of God by some other route. We cannot draw this concept out of finite events simply as finite.

Let us now return to John's doings. We observe that some of them are voluntary, others involuntary. He consents to some, but does not consent to others. He approves of some, disapproves of others. In some he is himself fully active, in others more or less passive. His will is expressed in purposive activity. He seeks to achieve various ends by the use of different available means. In some cases he makes a sustained and exhausting effort to achieve his objectives. In other cases he seems to achieve a measure of effortless self-expression. These latter activities he may be said to enjoy wholeheartedly for their own sake. But even on these occasions there is always room for improvement, some higher level of performance to attain. He may for a moment achieve a kind of perfection, but the moment passes, and the quest is renewed. This rhythm of seeking and enjoying and seeking again, of effort and attainment and renewed effort, is part and parcel of his being a person.

What happens when we use this sort of language to characterize the being of God? If we speak of the will of God, and define its objectives by reference to particular patterns of events in which his will is expressed, do we thereby imply that he is not active in other apparently incongruous patterns? Do these latter events occur without his consent, or even against his consent? Are we to say that he permits them, but does not constitute them? If this is the way in which we develop our language about God's activity, are we not imposing limitations on him which threaten his ultimacy and destroy his transcendence? Has he not been reduced to the ranks of finite beings?

On the other hand, if we persist with our assertion that God transcends the world, and if we wish to continue to speak of his creative activity in or over the world, rejecting the Aristotelian suggestion that God is only the final cause of the world and not the efficient cause, must we not then say that *everything* that happens is the expression of the divine will and activity? And if this is so, can we give any content to the concept of the divine will? Is there a pattern and purpose in everything that occurs, so that we can speak of its expressing the will of God? And if we can detect such an over-all pattern, does it extend to all the parts as well as to the whole? If not, is God limited by the means available to him in pursuit of his purposes, as a human craftsman is limited by the material with which he has to work? Or, again, if God's creative activity expresses itself in everything that occurs, on what grounds do we call him good? We should expect that his transcendent goodness would be reflected, if not in the best of all possible worlds, at least in a world that was transparently good of its kind and of a kind that was good —and yet, to say the least, this is by no means obviously the case.

The view which ascribes all events, destructive as well as creative, to the direct action of God certainly finds a place in the Bible. For example, it is God who hardens Pharaoh's heart. It is he who sends a lying spirit into the mouth of Zedekiah and his fellow-prophets, and raises up the Assyrians as the rod of his wrath to discard them when they no longer serves his purpose. He is the author both of good and of evil. It is not really surprising that so morally sensitive a philosopher as John Stuart Mill closed the book in dismay when he came to the verse in Isaiah: 'I form the light, and create darkness; I make peace, and create evil; I am the Lord that doeth all these things.'[18] If such is in fact the activity of God and the expression of his will, is he not a monster rather than the holy and righteous one?

Over against this view that God wills everything that occurs, the Bible also contains the view that human beings can and do rebel

[18] Isaiah 45.7.

against God, and that often they are guilty of actions which are *not* according to his will. They have before them the way of life and the way of death. It would be absurd to say that God is indifferent which choice they make, that it is all the same to him whether they choose life or whether they choose death. His will is declared in the offer of life. No doubt if they choose death, the death they choose can be interpreted as God's deliberate condemnation and punishment of their disobedience. The 'wrath of God' is nothing impersonal, if by this is meant some process of retribution outside and independent of his will. God is not a judge who dispenses rewards and punishments impartially and impersonally according to some ulterior law. He is not, first and foremost, a judge at all. He is the God whose will is most clearly expressed in acts of loving-kindness and mercy. We cannot conceive that he enjoys punishing as we can conceive that he enjoys forgiving. He is more himself when he saves than when he destroys. Divine punishment, if we are to retain the concept, stems from the dark side of God's being. But God is essentially light, not darkness.

The criticism may be levelled against us at this point that we have been developing personal language about God in a recklessly anthropomorphic manner which clearly reveals its latent but intrinsic absurdities. Now we need not deny that logical improprieties, if not absurdities, will arise when such personal language is used in this way. We have to remember that we are using our language analogously with reference to the transcendent God. Some of our more detailed analogies may illuminate, others may obscure. We cannot tell in advance which will be the case. We can only learn to discriminate as we use them. But underlying the use of personal language at all is the sense that in personal situations *par excellence*, that is, in situations in which men are conscious of exercising their own reflective freedom and responsibility, the apprehension of God is most likely to occur. And when this apprehension does occur a man is aware both of the presence of the transcendent God and of his coming to his own real self. 'I live; yet not I, but Christ lives in me,' says Paul. The second part of his confession corrects and completes but does not cancel the first part. In 'the paradox of grace' (to

E

borrow Donald Baillie's expression) a man apprehends the One who is the reality of his own being and yet at the same time gives him a reality of his own. Such is the apprehension of the condescension of God that language both of transcendence and of particularity is required even to begin to do it justice.

The biblical emphasis on the absolute freedom of God and on the relative freedom of man lends itself to a view of human history in which God's activity and man's are interwoven. God's will determines the ultimate course of events, but man has a real, though limited, power to direct the immediate course of events. The direction of the divine purpose is to be read off certain 'mighty acts of God', that is, off certain determinative events which are decisively apprehended as the expression of his will. These acts not only suggest the direction of God's will, they also hold out a promise of future fulfilment. Thus the apprehension of God's being and activity includes the faith that his purposes cannot ultimately be frustrated. As history runs its course, differing views come to be held concerning the objectives of these purposes and the manner of their fulfilment—now the conquest of Canaan, later the return from exile, then the coming of a second David to restore the glories of the first monarchy, culminating in hopes of a new era and finally of a new creation. God's purposes may be delayed by human disobedience, but they cannot finally be thwarted. Present faith and future hope are grounded in the conviction that the rule of God is both transcendent and providential.

When the transcendence of God is overlooked, language about God's purposive activity in history suggests that he is but one agent among many in the world. He is reduced to the status of finite being. Theological language becomes, in Bultmann's sense of the word, mythological. God's activity is interpreted in terms of this-worldly activity. Mythology 'speaks of gods as if they were men and of their actions as human actions, although it conceives of the gods as endowed with super-human power and of their actions as incalculable, as capable of breaking the normal, ordinary order of events'.[19] 'In

[19] Rudolf Bultmann, *Jesus Christ and Mythology*, London and New York 1960, p. 19.

mythological thinking the action of God, whether in nature, history, human fortune, or the inner life of the soul, is understood as an action which intervenes between the natural, or historical, or psychological course of events; it breaks and links them at the same time.'[20] That is, for mythology the action of God is of the same *order* as the action of men, however much it may differ in character.

The use of personal language to describe the activity of God cannot help presenting us with the problem of its interpretation. When it is understood in this context, the task of *'demythologizing'* is inescapable. It is part of the battle against the ever-present temptation of idolatry, of substituting some natural god for the transcendent Lord. But how is such interpretation to be effected? Must we discard all talk about the personal activity of God on the grounds that such talk is bound up with the particular spatio-temporal categories of the here and now? Or can we find refuge in talk of the constant, universal activity of God which sustains, but does not act within or intervene in, the changing world of space and time? If, however, we do justice by such a move to the transcendent being of God, may we not find ourselves driven in the long run to substitute impersonal language for personal?

We cannot deny the *prima facie* attractiveness of some form of deism. In fact, I would go further and venture the opinion that there must be a deistic element in any satisfactory Christian theology. I do not here have in mind the kind of deism which views the world as a perfect instance of cosmic engineering and then refers back to the cosmic Engineer who was in the beginning responsible for this intricate piece of work. Rather I have in mind a deism which, as it were, sets God back from his world and, without abandoning the ultimate dependence of all things upon his creative will, allows his world a relative independence. The world has room to be the world. It is not swallowed up in the divine being. In this way we may very properly speak of orders of nature and history which have a derivative being of their own and are open to natural and historical methods of interpretation without any reference to the activity of God. Natural scientists are able to discover more and

[20] Bultmann, *op. cit.*, p. 61. ·

more of nature's patterns. There is no need of the 'God-hypothesis' in order to make the work of the scientist coherent and intelligible. The same may be said about the pursuit of history. Historical methods of explanation do not include the activity of God. Historical events have their historical causes, and the historian's task is to lay bare the intricate patterns which hold together and explain the web of the historical process. Human purposes, motives, hopes and fears are the springs which turn the wheel of history. There is no place in the historian's vocabulary for the hand of God.

It is possible that there may be occurrences both in nature and in history that elude these kinds of explanation and do not fit into any discernible scientific pattern. Neither scientist nor historian need assert that the system which he builds must be completely closed. Nevertheless the whole success of their studies depends upon the search for such comprehensive systems, and more and more apparently stray pieces of the puzzle eventually find a place in their patterns. Consequently there is every justification for believing that there is a coherent order both in nature and in history which can be discovered by the methods of the natural and historical sciences.

If we are prepared to allow a real, though relative, independence to the world of nature and history, the effect upon religious belief is twofold.

In the first place it is no longer necessary to ascribe unusual and often destructive events to the immediate working of God. Earthquakes occur because of natural processes; they are not the acts of a God who intervenes in the normal course of affairs to express his displeasure and to punish the sinful. At the same time, however, it must be admitted that, if unusual and destructive events are the outcome of natural processes, so too are unusual and beneficial events. If a prolonged drought is to be understood as a natural occurrence and not a divine visitation, so too is the coming of the rain which ends the drought. If the onset of cancer is to be explained in natural terms, so too is its unforeseen remission. If the recognition of an order in nature enables us to say that ills are not sent by God, it also prompts us to say that blessings are none of his bounty either.

This brings us to the second point. It is still open to the believer to see the *whole* process of nature and the *whole* course of history as, in some sense, the work of God. God is then the transcendent 'cause' of all finite being. He does not intervene and make things different from what they are; he sustains and upholds them as they are. The whole pattern of rest and change, of advance and retreat, of light and darkness, of good and evil, is as he has made it. It is his will that it should be thus. It is his will that natural processes should work the way they do. It is his will that man should struggle in the midst of nature to establish a properly human form of life. It is his will that some should live in joy and misery. He has written the play, and so the play proceeds.

If, however, this is all that there is to be said about the being and activity of God, we must ask whether God is still the proper object of our worship? What manner of 'will' is his? Is the pattern of things so obviously good that we do well to praise its author? *Prima facie* attractive though deism is, the objection to it is that while it preserves the transcendence of God, it is morally and religiously as suspect as it is scientifically otiose. If the deistic God is to continue to engage our worship, we must have some positive assurance of his goodness. We must be assured of the value of his purpose and of the goodness of his will. We must be able to view the whole course of nature and of history from a vantage-point which will enable us to say 'yes' to it. Deism itself does not afford us this vantage-point.

There is a further objection. Let us assume that we have in fact discovered such a vantage-point, that we have made a positive evaluation of the direction of God's will, and that we keep this divinely-willed end in mind when we are planning our own actions and pursuing our own purposes. If God, as it were, has set the stage and determined the kind of play which he wishes his human actors to enact, but then has retired to the upper circle and allowed the drama to proceed as the actors wish, is there still any room for a living, personal relationship with God? If God helps those and only those who help themselves—if in fact his help is restricted to the conditions in which they are able to help themselves—then the whole language of God's help becomes irrelevant. It would be more honest to discard personal language altogether and to employ only impersonal analogies. The notion of the will of God has been deprived of all reference to a living, personal activity and has been transformed into something much closer to the impersonal concept of an unchanging, universal law or a constant, universal force.

In the chapter on 'God and the Particular' in his book *A Time for Christian Candour*, Bishop Pike uses four analogies to clarify the relation of the transcendent God to the particular event. First, a volcanic eruption. 'If a given spot becomes thin enough, soft enough, weak enough, that which underneath functions uniformly nevertheless manifests itself in a particular event.' Second, an oil-strike. 'A given corpus of oil does not decide to surface as a favour to an already opulent Texas millionaire. The oil is *there*; the oilman drills down to it and there is a strike.' Third, a central-heating system. 'When the knob is turned, something *happens*: the room begins to warm. But before, during, and after, the steam was acting with constancy. The heating system did not change; the situation in the room did.'[21] These three analogies are impersonal, and are peculiarly useful in stressing the universality and transcendence of God, and in suggesting one possible way of bridging 'the uniformity and speciality'.

Bishop Pike goes on to use a fourth analogy, that used by Jesus, the analogy of a perfect father. We are to assume that this perfect father is able to meet his children's needs, that he loves each and all of them completely and impartially and that he is eager to establish a living relationship with each. Now we may note that in this instance all these fatherly characteristics are assumed to be stable and unchanging. In this they are on a par with the impersonal characteristics of the previous analogies. In fact, human beings being what they are, impersonal analogies can often emphasize the features of constancy and stability more satisfactorily than personal analogies. But Bishop Pike is not content to leave the matter there. He writes: 'The Father would be less than personal if he were simply passive— just waiting to be called upon for what he can bring into any situation. In any contact in the dynamics of family life he has been open

[21] *Op. cit.*, p. 102.

from his direction; it is simply that there have been varying degrees of openness and closedness at various times on the part of his children—and he has not imposed his will.'[22] And he goes on to comment that this analogy is itself imperfect, 'since it is impossible to erase from our minds the finitude in even a virtually perfect father that would require positive individual decisions and actions in order for his general constancy to operate'.[23] The question which needs to be asked here is this. Is it the finitude inherent in the analogy even of a perfect father which makes us want to talk of his particular decisions, or is it the finitude actually inherent in the created children which suggests that even an 'infinite' father, if he is in a personal relationship with them, must be involved in something like individual decisions? Openness, loving-kindness, benevolence, as abstract qualities, are not the stuff of personal relationships. Acts of love, acts of kindness, acts of mercy are—and these acts are relative to the situations which call them forth. Must they not, then, be in some sense particular, even when they are the acts of an infinite Father, so long as they are directed towards finite and relatively independent children?

Let us pause here to take stock of the position which we have now reached. The religious sense of dependence which characterizes belief in God points to the mysterious transcendence of the God who is the object of such belief. His being is ultimate and universal. It remains beyond the reach of our ordinary conceptual apparatus. It demands a large measure of agnosticism. It suggests a *via negativa*. If something positive is to be affirmed about the being of God, it must be affirmed analogically. The most likely analogies seem to be those which are impersonal, since they preserve his universality. On the other hand, the biblical tradition, in speaking of a living God, makes use of personal analogies to describe his being and activity. The religious attitude which this tradition embodies is barely conceivable without the use of such personal analogies. In this lies both its strength and its weakness. Personal analogies are at the heart of biblical religion but are a stumbling-block to the philosophical mind. Thus reflection upon the biblical tradition oscillates

---

[22] *Op. cit.*, p. 103.   [23] *Op. cit.*, pp. 103f.

between agnosticism and anthropomorphism. Nevertheless, it refuses to jettison either the transcendence of God or his personal activity. Neither mode of speech is willing to give way to the other. Both claim an equal right to be heard.

We cannot claim to have solved the problem, but perhaps we have sharpened the issue. The movement towards transcendence in our thought about God suggests the propriety of impersonal rather than personal categories if we are to describe his being. The concept of the activity of God gives place to that of the realm of universal truth. The kingdom of God becomes the rule of law. The Incarnation of the Logos becomes the doctrine that God and man are at one. Prayer becomes meditation.

It seems that if we are to retain the Godness of God in opposition to all attempts to 'naturalize' him, we may be compelled to reject almost everything that is associated with the personal religion of the biblical tradition. On the other hand, the religion of the Bible obstinately refuses to be translated into impersonal categories. The living God refuses to be extruded from the world in which he is creatively and providentially active. His mysterious personal presence persists. We appear to have reached an *impasse*. But before we take the matter further, we must consider some of the objections to the religious sense of dependence upon God which arise from reflections on man's own personality and freedom.

Prayer and Action

THE movement towards transcendence in the development of theological understanding, the insistence that God is a supernatural and not a natural being, that he is the ultimate source and ground of all that happens and might happen, and that his activity surrounds, embraces and sustains all events equally within the empirical world, important and discerning as it is, nevertheless contains within itself a twofold threat.

The first threat, which we have already discussed, is the threat of meaninglessness. Theism tends towards deism. Deism tends towards agnosticism. And agnosticism concerning the ultimate loses itself in an all-absorbing concern with the penultimate. Or, to put the matter in a slightly different way, nature and history themselves become the two accepted 'ultimates'. The spirit of man confronts 'the inexorable forces of matter and chance', and endeavours in the incongruous episode of human life to come to terms with 'the benign indifference of the universe'.

The second threat is the threat to human freedom and values. On the one hand there is the question of the ontological status of human freedom. Is it not imperilled by theological transcendence even more than by physical determinism? Does not the notion of the all-embracing and all-sustaining activity of God degrade man into a divine plaything? Alternatively, if we wish to preserve the reality of human freedom and with this in mind go on to speak of the divine activity in radically personal rather than impersonal terms, do we not thereby detract from the transcendence of God by setting limitations to his activity? On the other hand there is the question, to which we have already alluded, of the goodness of God. Does the apparent indifference of the world to human values and ideals indicate a corresponding indifference in the being of God? And if this is the case, is there anything to be said in favour of the religious virtues of obedience and acceptance? Is not rebellion, or at least disdain, a more appropriate human response?

On these two topics we shall have something to say, first, concerning the goodness of God, and, second, concerning the moral ambivalence of religious acceptance.

To affirm that God is good immediately brings us face to face with the agonies of the world which cry out in contradiction of such an affirmation. Does God will the cataclysmic and lingering destruction of Hiroshima? Does he will the slow, painful death which can ensue upon the inexplicable growth of a cancer, or the imbecilities which can mark the onset and course of senile decay?

The believer may appeal to the limitations of human understanding in order to turn aside the full force of questions such as these and counsel acceptance of the will of God, whose thoughts and ways are ultimately incomprehensible to man. Alternatively he may attempt some form of theodicy. He may seek to pierce the darkness which surrounds God's ways and offer some explanation which can, at least in part, justify them at the bar of human conscience.

There are various types of theodicy which the believer may attempt, but despite their differences they all have a fundamental feature in common. They all set out to show that things are not quite what at first sight they seem to be. They suggest that, if we look at life in this way rather than in that, we shall see it in a different and more penetrating light. We shall see more of the picture than we had seen before, and our judgment will now reflect our greater understanding. Before we go any further, we must sound a warning. It is impossible to exaggerate the intellectual and moral peril which besets all theodicy. This lies in its insidious invitaton to us to blunt our sense of good and evil and to judge that things are not as bad as they seemed. The evils of Hiroshima, however, remain evil, whatever viewpoint we adopt. They do not vanish in some allegedly compensating harmony. There may be more to be said about them than the bare fact that they are evil, but the 'more' can never alter this bitter and ugly fact, or cause it by some dialectical cunning to disappear. We must be on our guard against any theodicy which evades the tragic depths of human life, and solves moral perplexities by distorting them and rendering them grotesquely superficial. Nevertheless, the world being what it is, and the believer's concept of the goodness of God being what it is, some form of theodicy has generally been thought desirable. If there has been doubt about its present possibility, there has been general agreement about its ultimate necessity. If God is the ultimate cause of all that happens in the world, what manner of God is he? Is he God or Devil?

Against this persistent desire to justify God's ways to man it may be asked whether the whole attempt to construct a theodicy is not a total mistake, both logically and religiously. Do we involve ourselves in utter confusion when we speak loosely of 'God's world'? Have we thereby introduced into our thinking the notion of a quasi-causal relation between God and the world when we ought to have interpreted the religious concept of the dependence of the world on God in some different, non-causal way? For example, it may be urged that we give expression to our sense of the dependence of the world on God when we thank him 'for everything', that is, when we express our gratitude for the whole complex pattern of life and our own part in it. God is not the cause of the good harvest rather than of the bad. He does not send the one rather than the other. In fact, it is misleading to use this language of personal agency at all. It suggests that God is pursuing some plan, that he carrying out some particular design within the world. But this is to limit God, to make him a part of the world. God is transcendent, supernatural, and we can express our sense of the dependence of the world on him by giving thanks that he is, by accepting the whole of life gladly in all its variegated colours, whatever combination of moral good and evil it may contain.

In *The Concept of Prayer*, D. Z. Phillips argues strongly that the whole idea of theodicy is bound up with the notion of a limited

God who is part of the world, and that its fundamental error is to treat God as a natural being, to fail to recognize the logical and religious implications of his supernatural character. He condemns as 'anthropomorphites' those, like Basil Mitchell and I. M. Crombie in their discussion with Antony Flew,[1] who think 'that God acts as we act, and that He can be held responsible for His actions as we are held responsible for ours'.[2] He argues that any appeal to final consequences in an attempt to persuade us to suspend moral judgment on God is bound to fail, because no consequences, however glorious, could justify some of the evils for which God is held to be ultimately responsible. 'No more need be said. God is condemned, for we believe that no consequences could justify torturing children to death. . . . Our morality passes judgement on the divine plan by showing how we, given the opportunity, would refuse to do what God is said to have already done.'[3]

Phillips makes a clear-cut distinction between morality and religion, and so between the basic human attitudes appropriate to either. Morality is, namely, expressed in action, religion in contemplation. Whatever our value judgments may be concerning the way things go in the world, these are, strictly speaking, irrelevant to the religious ascription of goodness to God. The religious affirmation that God is good is an expression of thanksgiving to God, an affirmation that life has meaning. 'To see the world as God's creation is to see meaning in life. This meaningfulness remains untouched by the evil in the world because it is not arrived at by an inference from it.'[4] 'The believer cannot expect one thing rather than another—in the world of events. The events do not constitute *evidence* for the goodness of God, since the essence of the believer's belief in the divine goodness consists precisely in the fact that the meaning of life does not depend on how it goes. . . . The naturalistic fallacy, from a believer's point of view, is to think that religion concerns *how* the world is.'[5] On the contrary, religion concerns the fact *that* the world is; and it is by contemplation of this

[1] See A. N. Flew and A. MacIntyre (eds.), *New Essays in Philosophical Theology*, London 1955, pp. 96ff.

[2] D. Z. Phillips, *The Concept of Prayer*, London 1965, p. 94.

[3] *Ibid.*   [4] *Op. cit.*, p. 97.   [5] *Op. cit.*, p. 102.

fact that religious devotion and thanksgiving to God may be engendered. 'Belief in God, possessing His spirit, is not contingent on what happens *in* the world, but is that which is given by contemplating *that* the world is and *that* there are other human beings, through the renunciation of the self.'[6] Self-renunciation is the way of finding meaning in life—not partial self-renunciation for the sake of a recognized good, but complete self-renunciation and acceptance of life as such. 'Love of God *is* sacrificial; it involves a denial of the self.'[7] 'Man has the spirit of God in him to the extent that he negates himself.'[8]

There is much that is attractive in this analysis of the religious sense of dependence on God, and Phillips' discussion deserves to be read *in toto*. First, it is true that the believer is urged by his fellow-believers to accept both good and ill as from the hand of God, to thank him at all times and for all things. Acceptance is certainly very close to the heart of the religious response. Second, to confess the faith that all things, including life's ills and accidents, come from God is certainly not to 'explain' them in the ordinary sense of explanation, as when we look for the empirical explanation of an event within the world. If God explains all things in this way, he explains nothing. Ordinary causal explanation employs the idea of something which causes this *and does not cause that*. To ascribe all things to God is to come to the end of explanation of this sort. In part, at any rate, it is to confess and counsel acceptance. Indeed, how often has it been said that Christian faith has no intellectual explanation of the facts of evil, but that it does offer a practical way of meeting and triumphing over them. On the suggested analysis of religious faith this is exactly what we should expect. Third, we may agree that there is no direct inference from the events of the world to the goodness of God. There is admittedly an element in religious faith which discounts the happenings in the world and urges adherence to God in spite of them. All these three points we have ourselves been anxious to stress in what we have said earlier.

Nevertheless, when all this is admitted, I cannot myself feel happy with an analysis which makes such sharp dichotomies be-

[6] *Op. cit.*, p. 105.   [7] *Op. cit.*, p. 100.   [8] *Op. cit.*, p. 101.

tween the *that* of the world and the *how* of the world, between the supernatural and the natural, or between religion and morality. The relation between the supernatural and the natural, or that between religion and morality, is notoriously problematical; but Phillips' analysis comes very close to denying that there is any significant relationship at all. In the first place, morality and religion seem for Phillips to be two unrelated ways in which man may respond to life. Each way of responding develops its own characteristic language and logic. Confusion must arise if the two languages are not kept separate. These two responses may both, it seems, be made by one and the same person. Such a combination is psychologically possible, but it is logically contingent. There can be no necessary connexion between them. Against this I should want to argue that one of the striking features of the biblical religious tradition, stemming from the witness of the prophets, is its interpretation of religion in essentially moral categories—or, if this is a somewhat misleading statement, we may prefer to speak of the unification of moral and religious analogies in the context of a relationship between God and man which, while transcending morality, neither ignores it nor negates it, but fulfils it. 'What doth the Lord require of thee, but to do justly, and to love mercy, and to walk humbly with thy God?'

In the second place, Phillips does not seem to do justice to the notion of the world's dependence on God. What, for him, does the religious affirmation of the dependence of the world on God amount to? God is to be praised because the world is, but not because the world is what it is. What the world is is irrelevant to the affirmation that God is. The goodness of God has nothing to do with the nature of the world, only with its existence and with a human way of responding to this existence. The world is dependent on God only in the sense that, whatever happens or does not happen, the believer may through self-renunciation express his own dependence on God. No evil occurrence can weigh against such self-renunciation. It is independent of worldly considerations. It would surely, then, be more appropriate to speak of the *believer's* sense of dependence

[9] Micah 6.8.

on God than of the *world's* dependence on God. The world simply is. To affirm that it is dependent on God is a very roundabout way of saying that it is to be accepted with self-renunciation. As against this it may be urged that language about the world's dependence on God has its origin and natural locus in the traditional belief that the world itself, as existing, raises the question and suggests the possibility of some metaphysical 'explanation'. And this may be found, according to one line of thought, in the idea of a Being who has created the world, and in whose perfect will resides the explanation both of the world's existence and of its ultimate nature.

God, however, is not only the maker of heaven and earth; he is also pre-eminently the source of all that is of value. The deepest human moral insights are a clue to the character of God. It is impossible to ignore what has been called 'the massive centrality' of morality in the biblical prophetic faith. God loves the good, and abhors the evil. Furthermore, God is to be trusted because he can be counted on to uphold the good. He is to be loved because he is worthy of human love. He seeks the good of his children. It is perfectly true that God's love is not conditioned by the goodness of his children. He loves impartiality. But this does not mean that he is indifferent to the evil in men or to the suffering that afflicts them. There is a lot of truth in the old saying that he hates the sin but loves the sinner. It is an attempt to set out the double character of divine love, its generosity and its righteousness. God loves the sinner despite his sin, but he is not benignly indifferent to his sin. Forgiveness is costly. Love not only accepts; it also judges and redeems.

We may, then, agree with Phillips that the religious response is one of acceptance, and that it is primarily nourished by contemplation of the One who is, rather than achieved by moral pursuit of that which ought to be. Nevertheless, such acceptance, at least from the biblical point of view, is grounded in the faith that there is some community of values between God and man. We might even speak of an *analogia boni*. Men are not invited to renounce themselves in favour of one who is indifferent to their own essential good, but to give themselves to him whom they can properly call 'Father'.

To call God 'Father' as well as 'Lord' is to confess a faith in his care for the happiness and well-being of his creatures, a care which must surely find *some* expression in the world he has created. This happiness and well-being is not to be equated with self-renunciation *tout court*, which is rather the rejection, not of self-centredness, but of the whole sphere of values as such, because they lead to discrimination between different parts and different aspects of creation. Whatever the logical and factual difficulties involved in talk about God's purposes in and with the world, it is at least an attempt to hold together the natural and the supernatural, the moral and the religious, in a manner which is more in keeping with the biblical tradition. 'The Lord is King, be the people never so impatient,' but he has still to establish his kingdom over all. It may be retorted that the New Testament marks a change from the naturalistic concept of God of the Old Testament, one who is involved in the establishment of an earthly kingdom, to a supernaturalistic concept of one whose kingdom is eternally present and can be entered by anyone who renounces himself for its sake; but it is doubtful whether all the evidence points in this direction. To put the same point in a different way, there remains throughout the New Testament a strand of futuristic eschatology in which there is to be a new heaven and a new earth, in expectation of which the whole created order waits in hope and travail. Such anticipation of the Not Yet, of which there are already signs and pledges, is, I believe, an ineradicable feature of Christian faith and hope. God is the God of the eternal present, but he is also the God of the temporal future. Such, I take it, is the significance of the doctrine of Christ's second coming.

It is almost impossible to exaggerate the importance of the dualistic element in the Bible, the conflict between God and the powers of this world. This dualism is never ultimate. The powers of this world are indeed of this world, and not original and uncreated. God remains the sole creator; beside him there is none other. Nevertheless, the conflict between the rule of God and the rule of Satan in the world is a real and terrible conflict. It is no mock affair with its outcome a foregone conclusion because it has been divinely rigged.

There is much that is contrary to God's positive will. He may permit, but he does not countenance or condone. Angels and men are in open rebellion against him.

What are we to make of the form of this mythology? Is it a sad naturalistic lapse from the high notion of the supernatural God who forms the light and creates darkness, who makes peace and creates evil? Is it a confusion of moral and religious terminology? Or are we to pay careful attention to the logic which underlies the mythology and which suggests that certain states of affairs reflect the mind and will of God more than others? If this logic is at all significant, we may proceed to develop our theological language in such a way as to assert that, while God actively sustains the whole created world, nevertheless his will is more fully expressed, he is 'more active', in some situations rather than in others.

This distinction of more and less in the activity of God has, I believe, an analogy in the human situation. For example, we sometimes say that John was 'more himself' in his behaviour today than he was yesterday. Yesterday the real John did not 'come through'. He was tired, or out of sorts. Things got on top of him, he was not his real self. Now we need not be crudely anthropomorphic by ascribing to God limitations in his own being such as we recognize in human beings. But limitations of a kind there must be, if we are to speak intelligently of a more and less; and these limitations, I suggest, must stem from the world which is the object of his creative activity. Consequently, this kind of language presupposes that the world which is absolutely dependent upon God has at the same time a measure of independence, a possibility of resisting the divine will. Thus we have something similar to what Barth has attempted to define in his paradoxical phrase 'the impossible possibility' of evil. Following this line of thought one may say that it is God's providential activity which is to be discerned in the way in which he meets and overcomes that which stands out against and resists his creative will. Here we see more of him than in any other situation. His activity meets with the creaturely response which it seeks and towards which it is directed. It is fulfilled in the response which it evokes. It penetrates and enables the relatively independent

F

activity of the creature. It supernaturalizes the natural. In such providential and redemptive activity we come to discern a deeper aspect
of God's being. There is a 'more' of God to be apprehended here
than elsewhere. His word speaks more clearly, his work is more
complete. Christians claim to discern such distinctive activity of God
in the life and work of Jesus. Thus on the cross, as he makes his
final, life-giving act of self-surrender to his Father, Jesus exclaims,
'It is finished,' and Christians ascribe in response to this a completion and finality to the divine work. Creator and creature are
here at one. The divine love has conquered. God remains eternally
the same God; but in and through the obedient response of Jesus
his activity is more fully discerned, because more fully expressed.
And since it is more fully expressed, there is a very proper sense in
which we may speak of God's *special* activity.[10] If the creature
ascends to the Creator, it is because the Creator has descended to
the creature. The Word has become flesh.

Correspondingly, the Christian believer, while exhorted to give
thanks to God always and for all things, since all things are in his
hand and ultimately dependent upon his will, can appropriately
single out certain things for special thanksgiving, for they embody
God's special activity. So we find in the words of the Prayer of
General Thanksgiving: 'We bless thee for our creation, preservation
and all the blessings of this life, but above all for thine inestimable
love in the redemption of the world through our Lord Jesus Christ,
for the means of grace, and for the hope of glory.' It is not only
that we find these things specially thankworthy; it is also that in
them we find God specially present.

This gives us a clue as to the grounds of our affirmation that
God is good. Certainly there is no ordinary inferential link between
what happens in the world and our assertion of the goodness of God.
As we have seen, such happenings are likely to suggest an ultimate
dualism rather than an ultimate theism. However, just as we have
argued earlier that belief in God involves a non-inferential appre-

---

[10] For an interesting development of this kind of argument see Schubert Ogden,
'What Sense does it Make to Say, "God Acts in History"?', in id., *The Reality of
God* and other Essays, London and New York 1967, pp. 164ff.

hension, a discernment of more than the empirical world, an awareness of that which transcends the objective world and confronts us
with a claim to worship, so we should argue that the Christian finds
this religious awareness and response mediated specially through a
particular series of events and a particular person in such a manner
that it purifies, deepens and transforms our moral sense of values. It
fulfils them rather than abrogates them. There is continuity as well
as discontinuity between the old and the new. Hence the religious
affirmation of the goodness of God is not unrelated to the moral
affirmation of human values. In this apprehension we ground our
trust in God. Such trust is not arbitrary. Nor is it at the expense of
our insights concerning moral goodness. It is certainly true that
the evil and suffering in the world may bring us to question the
validity of what we believe we have apprehended. They certainly
will count against our affirmation. Whether they will be counted
sufficient to disprove the validity of our affirmation will depend
upon the power of the initial confessed insight to renew itself in other
situations and to make sense of our other experiences. This cannot
be determined in advance. Faith is never logically secure. Although
it will incorporate a decision and may look suspiciously like the
adoption of an intransigent attitude in face of any and every empirical circumstance, it is not in fact an arbitrary decision, a leap in
the dark. It is a decision in the light of what it believes it has truly
apprehended concerning the ultimate character of the world.

Belief in God is belief in that which is ultimate, belief in him in
whom all things have their ultimate ground and explanation. The
concept of God is not only a religious concept but also a unifying
concept. It is tempting to treat religion as if it were after all only
one form of human activity among many. And so in some cases
it may be. But this, at least in the Christian tradition, is not its
proper character. It may be retorted that the demand for an over-all
unifying 'explanation' of our many different kinds of experience
is a piece of mistaken metaphysic rather than of true religion. I do
not believe this to be the case. I believe that it is of the essence of the
Christian religion always to generate a unifying world-view, to try
to bring into some sort of harmony our different spheres of

experience. It may never succeed, but it must never abandon the attempt. If this is indeed the case, then some form of theodicy is inescapable. If we introduce the concepts of the mind and will of God as unifying concepts, they must be capable, at least in principle, of unifying our experiences of nature and of man. We may never do more than sketch certain ways in which such a unification might possibly be effected; but if we are convinced that there is no such unity to be discovered, then we have abandoned belief in the biblical God. There will always be a place in Christian theology for the visionary like Irenaeus or Teilhard de Chardin who seeks to trace the thread of God's creative purpose running through the whole course of nature and history. We cannot discover or establish the activity of God in nature and history in any empirical manner. The natural and the historical sciences as such do not and cannot operate with such a concept. It is foreign to their procedures. But if we have other grounds for speaking of the activity of God, and of his purpose and will, there is no logical reason why we should not believe that God is 'working his purpose out' in nature and seek to discern signs of this activity. This readiness to discern signs derives from a prior faith in the activity of God and some prior understanding of the character and direction of this activity; it does not seek evidence which will prove that God is active. No such proof is possible. This is part of what is meant by those who speak of the 'hiddenness' of God in nature and history. But his hiddenness is not to be equated with his absence. So much is admitted even by Bultmann, whose main thesis is that the mythological statements of the Bible should be interpreted existentially rather than cosmologically, and that we come to know and apprehend the action of God only here and now as we ourselves are confronted by his word, which challenges our self-understanding and self-determination. He writes: 'God's action generally, in nature and history, is hidden from the believer just as much as from the non-believer. But in so far as he sees what comes upon him here and now in the light of the divine word, he can and must take it as God's action. Pantheism can say "there divinity is working" with regard to any event, whatever it may be, without taking into account the importance of what happens for my personal existence. Christian faith can only say, "I trust that God is working here and there, but His action is hidden, for it is not directly identical with the visible event. What it is that He is doing I do not yet know, and perhaps I shall never know it, but faithfully I trust that it is important for my personal existence, and I must ask what it is that God says to me. Perhaps it may be only that I must endure and be silent." [11] Thus faith in God's activity, which I apprehend here and now, may extend to faith in his activity in the world, although this faith remains faith and not knowledge, and God's activity in the world remains objectively hidden.

We turn now to consider what I have called the moral ambivalence of religious acceptance.

We have agreed that the heart of the religious response to life is, in some sense of the word, acceptance. Life is to be accepted because it comes to man from the hand of God. But what precisely does such acceptance involve? One of the sharpest attacks against religion has been made in the conviction that such religious acceptance is morally deleterious, that it fails to do justice either to human dignity or to the challenge and possibility of changing the world for the better rather than accepting it as it is. *'Tantum religio potuit suadere malorum.'* Religion is condemned as opium. The accusation is made that it breeds contentment when moral sensitivity demands discontent. It meets the challenge of human needs and longings with a determined attempt to suppress them rather than to fulfil them. Its attitude to life is one of denial. It is a continual 'Nay-saying, Nay-doing'. Surrender to God is the surrender of man's very humanity, of his freedom and his rationality. The religious response is typified in the exhortation which the Jesuit gave to John Inglesant when he was training him for his future mission to abet the return of England to the catholic faith: 'We have been placed here not to reason (as the sectaries do), but to obey.' Unquestioning obedience to the divine command is the religious order of the day. Furthermore, the religious attitude finds, perhaps, its most pernicious expression in its glorification of suffering. Suffering is extolled pre-

[11] R. Bultmann, *Jesus Christ and Mythology*, p. 64.

cisely because it provides the supreme example of self-denial.

One does not have to commit oneself to the excesses of a Nietzsche to be persuaded that an attitude which has no place for human values and human fulfilment is an attitude to be rejected in the name of humanity. There are many, including in their number men of a religious frame of mind, who would claim to see in man's freedom over against the world, his moral responsibility and his powers of self-determination, the starting-point for any convincing philosophy of life. In the name of human freedom, however, some have been convinced of the necessity of denying God. The non-existence of God becomes the *conditio sine qua non* of a viable humanism. Religion is bondage most vile: man achieves his liberty only through its utter rejection.

Full force must be given to sentiments such as these. Mutterings about the original sin of human pride are beside the point. It may well be man's continual temptation and error to believe that he occupies the centre of the stage, and that his own interests and concerns are the predominant feature of the universe. It may be equally erroneous, however, to believe that these have no place on the stage at all. Nor is it true to say that the Christian tradition has always been anti-humanistic, or that its interpretation of the religious value of self-surrender and self-denial has always been destructive of human endeavour. Self-sacrifice can be seen as part and parcel of more abundant life, the service of God as itself the discovery of perfect freedom. Self-surrender and freedom may appear to be antithetical notions, and in some instances they clearly are antithetical. But this is not always so. For example, in a mutual relationship of friendship or of love there is both a giving and a receiving which enhances the freedom and responsibility of those involved. Something similar may be claimed when it comes to man's surrender to God. The Christian believes that this surrender can be made with complete trust and confidence because the God to whom he surrenders himself wills to bring him to his full freedom and humanity. In fact he is 'wont to give more than we either desire or deserve'. We love—and love involves acceptance and sacrifice—because he first loved us.

There is a further point to be made concerning the relationship of love between God and man. It can best be introduced by thinking again of the relationship of human love. In deeply loving human relationships we discover what we may call an interpenetration of personal being. I and Thou become a We in which the boundaries of the I and Thou are subtly extended, so that it becomes increasingly difficult to distinguish sharply between the I and the Thou. The lover and the beloved develop an integrating and integrated responsiveness and responsibility. The one lives in and through the other. At the same time the one is not swamped by the other. There is an enhancement of the being of both. This is in marked contrast to the being of material objects. No two things can occupy the same physical space. There is an exclusiveness about material being. Two persons, however, can to a certain extent occupy the same spiritual space. Personal being exhibits the quality of inclusiveness, of identity-in-difference. Certainly this interpenetration of man's personal being in love must not be exaggerated. There seems to be a centre to man's personal being which is impenetrable by another person. Nevertheless, interpenetration of personal being I take to be a fact of human experience.

With this analogy in mind we may now consider the relationship between God and man in terms of personal love. The religious sense of participation in divine being is faced with the problem of preserving the reality of human freedom. It is here that the human analogy of love may suggest a solution. Participation in divine being may be understood in terms of personal interpenetration. The divine love moves towards a *total* interpenetration of the human creature. The believer surrenders himself without reserve to God, who wills to become all in all. But this in-allness of God enhances the human person, does not absorb or destroy it. All is of grace; and because grace is the grace of love, I become myself and find my freedom.

> The sweetest wife on sweetest marriage-day,
>   Their souls at grapple in mid-way,
>   Sweet to her sweet may say:

'I take you to my inmost heart, my true!'
Ah, fool! but there is one heart you
  Shall never take him to!

The hold that falls not when the town is got,
The heart's heart, whose immured plot
  Hath keys yourself keeps not! . . .

Its keys are at the cincture hung of God;
Its gates are trepidant to His nod:
  By Him its floors are trod.[12]

If, then, we are to avoid the moral dilemmas awaiting the unwary who without more ado endorse a religious attitude of self-surrender, we must preserve an important place for human freedom in our understanding of what is signified by dependence on God. The religious response will be one of working with God as well as one of waiting upon God. While we may accept wholeheartedly Tillich's declaration that 'the usual question, "What shall we do?" must be answered with the unusual question, "Whence can we receive?",[13] we cannot divorce this receptivity from our activity. The assertion of the ultimacy of God has as its corollary the assertion that human being, as all creaturely being, is fundamentally receptive. 'All things come from thee, O Lord, and of thine own have we offered thee.' The grace of God is all-sufficient, prevenient as well as accompanying. Nevertheless, the parallel assertion of the importance of human personality and freedom prompts us to interpret this receptivity in such a way that it makes room for, in fact demands and sustains, human freedom and activity.

The ascription of personality to God is a determined attempt to hold together the religious and moral sides of human life in a unity, since it is in inter-personal relations that we discern the possibility of a harmony of giving and receiving, of acceptance and activity. It is in the intercourse of love that it becomes possible to accept a person as he is and at the same time to evoke in him the desire and ability to become what he potentially is. This double theme of being and

[12] Francis Thompson, *A Fallen Yew*, quoted by John Baillie, *And The Life Everlasting*, Oxford 1934, p. 57.
[13] P. Tillich, *The Protestant Era*, London 1951, pp. 184f.

becoming is characteristic of the Christian idea of salvation. Thus in the seminal thought of St Paul we find a recurring tension between salvation as a present reality and as a future hope, between the proclamation of the gospel of forgiveness and the summons to realize to their full extent the implications for life and behaviour of this newly established divine-human relationship. Believers are to become what they already are. Born of the Spirit they are to walk by the Spirit. Autobiographically St Paul himself writes: 'Not that I have already obtained, or am already made perfect: but I press on, if so be that I may apprehend that for which also I was apprehended by Christ Jesus. Brethren, I count not myself yet to have apprehended: but one thing I do, forgetting the things which are behind, and stretching forward to the things which are before, I press on toward the goal unto the prize of the high calling of God in Christ Jesus.'[14]

We are now in a better position to understand the ambivalence present in the religious notion of acceptance. A sense of communion with God will lead a man to view the whole of life as originating from his creative will and to accept it as from his hands. At the same time it will include a recognition of the fact that there is much in life which is contrary to God's will and will give rise to an active struggle against this evil. This combination of activity and passivity finds succinct expression in the prayer attributed to Reinhold Niebuhr: 'God, grant me the serenity to accept the things I cannot change, the courage to change the things I can, and the wisdom to know the difference.' But the fullest and finest expression of which I am aware is to be found in Teilhard de Chardin's classic, *Le Milieu Divin*, and I do not hesitate to quote at length from this profoundly sensitive and perceptive work:

'When a Christian suffers, he says "God has touched me". The words are pre-eminently true, though their simplicity summarizes a very complex series of spiritual operations; and it is *only when we have gone right through the whole series of operations* that we have the right to speak these words. For if, in the course of our encounters with evil, we try to distinguish what the Schoolmen

[14] Philippians, 3.12-14.

term "the instants of nature", we shall have, on the contrary, to begin by saying "God wants to free me from this diminishment—God wants me to help Him to take this cup from me". To struggle against evil and to reduce to a minimum even the ordinary physical evil which threatens us, is unquestionably the first act of our Father who is in heaven; it would be impossible to conceive Him in any other way, and still more impossible to love Him. . . . At the first approach of the diminishments we cannot hope to find God except by loathing what is coming upon us and doing our best to avoid it. The more we repel suffering at the moment, with our whole heart and our whole strength, the more closely we cleave to the heart and action of God.'[15] 'Unless I do everything I can to advance or resist, I shall not find myself at *the required point*—I shall not submit to God as much as I might have done or as much as He wishes. If on the contrary, I persevere courageously, I shall rejoin God across evil, deeper down than evil; I shall draw close to Him; and at that moment the optimum of my "communion in resignation" neces-sarily coincides (by definition) with the maximum of fidelity to the human task.'[16] In putting the question what a Christian ought to prefer, activity or passivity, possession or renunciation, Teilhard de Chardin summarizes his answer in the following striking way: 'Why separate and contrast the two natural phases of a single effort? Your essential duty and desire is to be united with God. But in order to be united, you must first of all *be*—be yourself as com-pletely as possible. And so you must develop yourself and take possession of the world *in order to be*. Once this has been accomp-lished, then is the time to think about renunciation; then is the time to accept diminishment for the sake of *being in another*. Such is the sole and twofold precept of complete Christian asceticism.'[17]

Understood in this way communion with God is a developing spiritual process which will take different forms in different situa-tions. Correspondingly God will be conceived as calling for dif-ferent responses at different times—now activity, now passivity, now

[15] Pierre Teilhard de Chardin, *Le Milieu Divin*, London 1960, pp. 62f.
[16] *Op. cit.*, p. 73.
[17] *Op. cit.*, p. 78.

self-development, now self-surrender. The particularity of every situation will have a corresponding particularity in the will of God. His unchanging and unchangeable love will wear a variety of faces. Response to this love, and a deepening sense of communion with God, may lead a man along a strange odyssey. If he has to become himself before he can truly surrender himself, it may also happen that he cannot truly praise God for the blessings of this life until he has reached and passed the point of blaming him for its ills, or that he cannot fully make his own the forgiveness of God until he has 'forgiven' God himself. The words of self-surrender, 'Father, into thy hands I commend my spirit,' take on a new depth of meaning when they are seen in close conjunction with the cry of dereliction, 'My God, my God, why hast thou forsaken me?'

We may pause here and take stock of the ground on which we are standing when we begin to formulate our belief in God's providential activity in the world.

First, this belief is not a limited empirical hypothesis put forward to account for certain features of the world as against other features. It is much more like a way of seeing the world as a whole, a seeing which is held to do justice not only to the empirical facts, but also to that which is apprehended as transcending these facts and which evokes an appropriate response of worship. Nor is this belief derived from some postulate of idealistic logic which asserts that everything must be rational and therefore that everything must be good. Evil still remains evil. It cannot be explained away into something other than it is. Doubtless there is something noble, but there is also something strangely perverse, about the stoic Posidonius's exclamation when he was racked with pain: 'It's no use, pain. No matter how you attack me, I will never admit that you are evil.'[18]

Secondly, it is this moral discrimination between good and evil which inclines us to the view that certain occurrences in the world cannot accord with the will of God, despite the fact that he is the ultimate reality upon which all else depends. We are tempted to say that, although he may permit these occurrences, they do not

---

[18] Posidonius, in Cicero, *Tusculan Disputations*, II, 25, 61.

express his positive will. Despite the ultimate dependence of all things upon God, the world must possess a peculiar mode of independence.

Plainly, such a distinction between the permissive and positive will of God threatens his ultimacy and transcendence. It might therefore seem more appropriate to use the impersonal analogy of law rather than the personal analogy of will when speaking of the relation of the imperfection and evil in the world to that transcendent being in the light of which it is judged imperfect and evil. This law would be universal and unchanging, permanent and unlimited. Certain features of the empirical world would reflect this divine law more than others. Some would be in accordance with it, others contrary to it. Human beings might discern this law, and seek to organize their own lives and that of the world in obedience to it. They might feel a religious reverence for this law, and exercise their freedom in conformity with it. No doubt there would be various problems about the ontological status of an ultimate 'law'. Even so, the more or less impersonal analogy of law avoids many of the problems confronting the use of the personal analogy of the will of God, some of which have been occupying our attention. Is it possible, for example, to retain the distinctive transcendence of God and still to speak of his will? A God who willed something, but never acted in any way to express his will, would be a strange God indeed. The concepts of will and activity are correlative and cannot easily be separated.

Thirdly, Christian apprehension of God is associated with a particular person, Jesus Christ. It is the understanding of his life which defines and controls the Christian understanding of the being of God. The heart of the gospel of Christ is the forgiveness of sins, to be interpreted not in some negative or narrow manner, but in the sense of the overcoming of that alienation in human life which is called sin. Man cannot by his own free activity overcome this alienation. He is divided in himself. He is free, and yet he is not free. At the heart of the Christian proclamation is the good news that what man cannot do of himself has been done and can be done for him. This new self-understanding, this healing of his personal being, this restored relationship with that which constitutes and fashions his own life, comes to him as a gift. He receives the forgiveness of his sins. To speak of this restoration and renewal of his personal being the language of personal love is well-nigh unavoidable. If it is true to say 'I am, because I am loved', then the forgiveness of sins is naturally described as the outcome of the redemptive activity of divine love. Love is essentially active, and it is directed towards the particular object of its care. It is impossible to be loving in general without actually loving in particular. It is impossible to have the quality of love without exercising the activity of love. Hence the providential activity of God is seen pre-eminently in man's reconciliation through Jesus Christ to the ultimate source of all life in which he himself participates as a personal being.

Fourthly, the context in which this forgiveness of sins and renewal of personal life is set is a context which embraces both history and nature. It is a cardinal error to divorce the individual from his relations to other men, from his cultural history, and from his natural origins. Although he transcends his environment and his origins, he cannot disown them. Although the gospel of Jesus Christ may in the first place be appropriated existentially as a gospel of the forgiveness of an individual's own sin, it cannot rest there, but must realize itself as also a gospel of God's creative and providential activity in nature and history. Jesus is Redeemer, but he is also Lord. There has been a *praeparatio evangelica*, and there will also be a *parousia*, in which God will be all in all, the measure of his will expressed and reflected throughout the whole of his creation. Both the essence of human personality and the character of God compel the Christian to extend the language of divine activity beyond the confines of individual existence. It is perfectly proper for him to speak of God's activity in nature and in history in spite of the fact that he is ignorant of its manner and may mis-read the signs of its presence. To use such language is not a symptom of an archaic mythology which treats God as if he were a part of the world. It derives from the very structure of his apprehension of the divine presence. In this regard, G. Wingren's criticism of Bultmannian theology touches the nerve of the argument. 'To demy-

thologise the Gospel in such a way means to lose the possibility of
speaking about the dealings which God and Jesus Christ have with
all men, dealings which embrace the whole of life and in which the
redemptive act on behalf of the individual has its proper though
subsequent place. When the principal emphasis comes to be laid
on what God does for the individual, those biblical passages which
plainly set forth what He has done or will do for all men at Calvary,
Easter, the *parousia*, and the last judgment, are inevitably given a
subordinate place through some kind of anthropological interpretation to the immediate response of the individual to the *kerygma* in
face of the onset of his death. The fundamental error in this existential view is not that it does away with miracles, but that it gives
a quite mistaken prominence to the individual.'[19]

Fifthly, and finally, because the Christian sees his own life, not in
isolation, but in intimate relation both to history and to nature, and
because his apprehension of God is a cosmic rather than a partial
apprehension, so his hope, springing from his faith in God's
presence, is not simply hope against hope, that is, an irrational com-
pensation for a deep intellectual despair, but hope in a future consummation in which God will bring all things into conformity with
his will. It is the hope of glory. The new life into which the Christian
believer is initiated is only the beginning of a new life for the whole
created order. The pattern and the power of this new life are to be
discerned in Jesus Christ. In him faith acknowledges an unbroken
participation in the being of God and it acclaims an undistorted expression of the divine will and activity. But the fullness of the new
life is not yet. It is still to come. It lies in a future age, when there
will be 'a new heaven and a new earth'. It is not possible to say
much more than this. We barely sense what it is that we are saying.
We wonder whether we are saying anything at all. We are trans-
gressing the bounds of understanding. Our imagination, too, fails
us. Nevertheless, we dare not say less than this. If God is God, if
our apprehension of his being has not been a delusion, then present
faith must be balanced by a future hope which, pointing beyond the
world as we know it, is nevertheless the outcome and perfection of

that world. The Christian believes that it is open to faith to be grasped by the power of the new age here and now. His communion with God is present participation. At the same time it is also anticipation of the *parousia*.

V

With God in the World

CHRISTIANS believe that the world has its ultimate ground and explanation in the will of God. He is its alpha and omega, its origin and its goal. His will has found its fullest expression in the person of Jesus Christ, in whose response to the circumstances which provided the context and material of his life we have an insight into the character of the divine will. We mark both the congruity and the responsiveness of Jesus' will to the will of God by the affirmation that in him the divine Word became flesh. The Fourth Gospel can be read as a meditation on this communion between Jesus and God, a communion both of waiting and of working, a communion which, while preserving the humanity of Jesus, was so complete that it demanded the language of unity. 'The Father is greater than I.' 'I and the Father are one.'

Not only was the direction of the divine will expressed in Jesus Christ, but its purpose, at least in principle and in part, was achieved. There may be many divine purposes embodied in his creation of the world; but one at least we take to be the creation of beings who freely and consciously respond to his own creative love in a living communion. Such a response, it is affirmed, was the response of Jesus, embodied in his life and completed in his death. 'Son though he was, he learned obedience in the school of suffering, and, once perfected, became the source of eternal salvation for all who obey him.'[1] What was achieved in one man, however, was not yet the

---

[1] Hebrews 5.8f. (NEB).

fullness of God's will. Jesus was to be the first of many, the author
and pioneer of a way of life along which all men were invited to
follow. By the light of apprehension and through the response of
faith a man may already participate in the divine-human life which
is the life of Christ. He may already enter into a fellowship of the
spirit, dying to his former disrupted life of self and sin and raised
to the new life of God and charity. He may become, by adoption,
son of God and joint-heir with Christ. Language such as this, meta-
phorical as it obviously is, claims that in that area of self-understanding and self-determination in which a person is constituted a person
something new and recreative has taken place. 'The only thing that
counts is new creation.'[2] In the presence of God and through the
action of God he becomes a new being. In losing himself in the love
of God he finds himself.

Nevertheless, this 'already' exists in a tension with an equally real
'not yet'. The believer still belongs, very obviously, to the same
imperfect and distorted world as before. He is himself still involved
in the struggle with himself, *simul iustus et peccator*. There are
many other spirits, besides the spirit of God, which make him what
he is—the spirit of the age, of his family and class. He is still a son
of Adam. Consequently his faith exists in the tension between the
'already' and the 'not yet'. Salvation is a future hope as well as a
present foretaste. In fact hope colours the nature of his faith: he
looks forward to what lies ahead with confidence. The future is
not governed by fate or chance, it is God's future.

What does the believer hope for? When we discount the obviously imaginative features with which every doctrine of the *parousia*
clothes itself, we can, I think, discern three inter-related aspects of
this future hope.

First, it looks forward to a time when the believer will no longer
be divided within himself by the conflict between grace and sin,
between God's perfect love for him and his own imperfect response
to the love of God. Not only will he find confirmation of the veracity
of his apprehension of the being of God (an apprehension which in
this life is of the nature of faith rather than of sight), such that

[2] Galatians 6.15 (NEB).

G

communion with God will no longer be partial and intermittent but stable and all-pervasive, deepening and enlightening his whole experience; but he will also find that this communion is what it has become because it is part of a total response embracing his whole personal being, a response of love unbroken by sin. He will know as he has been known, because he will love as he has loved.

Second, because his own personal being is in part constituted by relationships with other persons, the believer will look forward to a communion of saints, in which participation in the divine life will find expression in a participation in the life of other finite persons. He will find his own true being in the love of God *and* the love of neighbour. No longer will there be destructive divisions within the body of Christ; these will yield to a mutual support and edification in the power of the divine love. 'So shall we all at last attain to the unity inherent in our faith and knowledge of the Son of God. . . . He is the head, and on him the whole body depends. Bonded and knit together by every constituent joint, the whole frame grows through the due activity of each part, and builds itself up in love.'[3]

Third, the future hope includes the resurrection of the body. Now finite personal existence is existence-in-the-world. Subjectivity is directed towards an object. There is a common world which provides material for personal interest and concern and for interpersonal communication. Out of this world human society and human nature have evolved. Although transcending nature, human beings are also the products of nature. Consequently a future which is sufficiently continuous with the present to be called the fulfilment and perfection of the present will include not only persons in community but also a common 'world'. There will be 'a new heaven and a new earth', both continuity and discontinuity with the present heaven and earth. This resurrection body will express in its own perfect way, as nature now barely and imperfectly expresses, the activity of the divine love, and it will at the same time be the harmonious medium for the expression, in response to the same divine love, of fully personal human relationships. Nature and man to-

[3] Ephesians 4.13, 16 (NEB).

gether will find their fulfilment in the peace of God. 'The wolf shall dwell with the lamb, and the leopard shall lie down with the kid; and the calf and the young lion and the fatling together; and a little child shall lead them. . . . They shall not hurt nor destroy in all my holy mountain: for the earth shall be full of the knowledge of the Lord, as the waters cover the sea.'[4]

It may be said that we have taken biblical mythology too literally, and that the dimensions of Christian hope should be reduced to the area of the individual's authentic self-understanding within the confines of birth and death. In this area at any rate we can have some claim to know what we are talking about! There are too many issues involved here to permit a sustained discussion. All I can do now is to give voice to my own conviction that, despite a very proper caution and a healthy modicum of agnosticism, the logic of the New Testament proclamation and the logic of Christian hope both demand that we refuse to accept the limitations imposed upon us by our experience in this life as ultimate. If it is the character of personal being which affords us our least inadequate clue to the ultimate being and will of God, then this same clue, supported by the proclamation that Jesus Christ was raised from the dead, prompts us to hope that, although in so many ways products of nature, persons are nevertheless not completely the playthings of nature. The dissolution of the flesh is not necessarily the destruction of the human person.

These, then, are the marks of the Christian hope in a *parousia*, in an open rule of God. Now prayer, as we suggested at the close of our last lecture, is in part an anticipation of the *parousia*, an adherence in the present to that which it is believed and hoped will be realized in the future. We can wholeheartedly endorse R. Gregor Smith's fine description of prayer in the striking appendix to his book *Secular Christianity*, even though we dissent from his existentialist reduction of the Christian proclamation and his diminution of the fullness of the Christian hope. He writes that prayer is 'to be understood as the anticipation in the whole of our existence of that one End which is the reality of God. . . . Not an attitude or a formula, it is not a content and not even a form. But it is the engagement of

[4] Isaiah 11.6, 9.

the whole life in the hope of the End in Christ.'[5] That is, prayer is the anticipation here and now of that fulfilment of God's purpose for the world which the Christian hopes for and expects at the *parousia*. It is the inward process by which the end-time, inaugurated by Jesus Christ, is hastened towards its consummation. It is the spiritual bond between the 'already' and the 'not yet'. It is also the bridge between belief and works. As Martin Thornton rightly points out, 'moral action only flows from doctrinal truth by grace and faith, that is *through* prayer'.[6]

Just as this future hope develops out of faith in Jesus Christ as the full expression in human life of the divine will and action—in him God's kingly rule prevails, and in him we acknowledge both the fact and the manner of the divine activity, so that he is 'himself the kingdom' (*autobasileia*)—so too the anticipation of this future hope in prayer derives from a faith in the power of God to use our prayer for the furthering of his purposes. It is no compulsive figment of the imagination by which we pretend that things are not what they really are, and dream that they might be what we should like them to be. It is a contemplation of their present actuality within the context of the reality of the eternal purposes of God, such as we have reason to believe these to be. It is a seeing of the world and of our neighbour in the light of the new creation in Christ and in the confidence that the spirit of God lays hold upon our spirit and informs our hearts and minds. In prayer we learn to participate in the mind and action of God. St Paul very truly remarks that 'we do not even know how we ought to pray', but he continues with the confident assurance that 'the Spirit himself is pleading for us . . . and in everything, as we know, he co-operates for good with those who love God and are called according to his purpose'.[7] Because it flows from a recognition of what God has already done in and through Jesus Christ, prayer will always have the note of thanksgiving. Because it looks forward to what God has still to do in and through those who respond to his love, it will also have the note

[5] R. Gregor Smith, *Secular Christianity*, London 1966, p. 208.
[6] M. Thornton, *The Rock and the River*, London 1965, p. 20.
[7] Romans 8.26, 28 (NEB).

of petition and intercession. It has often been remarked that petitionary prayer is to be found at the centre of Christian communion with
God. The reason for this should be clear if we keep in mind, first, the
tension between the 'already' and the 'not yet', and, second, the co-
operation which God seeks from man in the pursuit of his purposes.
Petitionary prayer can then be seen for what it is, namely, the
confluence of divine providence with human faith. Activity and
passivity combine. Prayer is both a resting in God and a wrestling
with God. In its essential character communion with God is not a
participation of the senses in the processes of nature. Nor is it a
submission of the mind to a rational necessity which determines all
that happens. Man protests in the name of his moral and personal
freedom against such would-be divinities. Christian faith, however,
claims that communion with God and self-surrender to his will is to
be found on the other side of moral protest, for it discovers that
dependence upon God and participation in the divine life is a
dependence on a Love which gives man his freedom and does not
destroy it. Man's own being is penetrated by the being of God, yet
without diminishment. The indwelling of God is the condition of
his self-fulfilment.

Just as we have insisted that Christian prayer is an anticipation
of the *parousia*, so we must remember that it is only an anticipation.
Christian prayer as well as Christian life is involved in and conditioned by the actualities of the world as it is. There is no magical
transformation which ignores the conditions of history and of
nature as they have come to be. There is in prayer itself the same
tension between the 'already' and the 'not yet' as we have seen
in the rest of Christian experience. The believer's offering of prayer
is not yet the perfect response to God of obedience, wisdom and love.
He offers it, therefore, in the name of the One whose response was
perfect. He associates his offering with the perfect offering of Christ.
In this way he expresses his faith both in the once-and-for-all
achievement of Jesus Christ and in the continuing activity of his
spirit. Although this faith comes to him as a gift—that is, he himself is unable to control the initial apprehension and response of
faith—nevertheless the response demanded by this initial apprehen-

sion includes an active perseverance in the direction in which this faith points. The powers of the human will are liberated rather than set aside. Passivity and activity once again combine. And because of the tension between the 'already' and the 'not yet' a deliberate persistence in prayer is as important as a heart-felt but transient desire to pray. God is 'more ready to hear than we to pray'. A disposition to pray, or a habitual recollection of God, is developed by determinate and deliberate acts of prayer. These latter need not substitute a regimen of duties for an adventure of love, as love itself knows and creates its own disciplines. Spontaneity and order are mutually self-supporting.

Anticipation of the End in God through prayer is no substitute for the determined attempt to give expression to that reality in the situation in which we find ourselves. Prayer is no substitute for work. If it is a mistake to think of prayer merely as a technique for the better performance of one's work, since communion with God is an end in itself and not simply a means to some other end, it is equally mistaken to think that communion with God can develop and deepen without an active concern for God's purposes in the world. If we think it is correct to speak at all of God's purposes in the world, purposes which have yet to be fulfilled, then communion with God will include co-operation with God. The situation in which we find ourselves when we turn to prayer is the point at which our co-operation is required. This situation will provide part of the material for our prayer as well as the immediate context in which prayer is continued in work. God calls us to be his fellow-workers, to participate in his ongoing activity in the world. Although it would be a mistake to blur the distinction between prayer and work—in prayer we focus our attention upon the ultimate, the being and will of God, and see the penultimate in relation to the ultimate, while in work we focus our attention upon the penultimate, and although we may retain the spirit of God in our hearts, we no longer have him before our minds—we may nevertheless agree that prayer and work are two poles of a single response to God. 'To rely on science and human technique to get what we want, without prayer, is irreligious. . . . But to pray without doing what we can to secure what we pray for, in accordance with the best knowledge we possess, is futile; and to worship God without reference to what he has done and is doing in the world, is not to worship the true God at all.'[14] We are to take our place with God in the world, allowing his love to shape and direct our actions in the world, and so to express and further his activity in the world. We are also to take our place before God, when it is God rather than the world who occupies the centre of our attention.

Perhaps we may here be allowed a short digression from the main course of our argument in order to say something more about the two kinds of relationship which I have called 'with God' and 'before God'. I conceive them both as forms of personal relationship, that is, of a relationship in which a man can express his being as a person and not merely as an object. To be before God is to experience communion with God as a 'face-to-face' relationship, similar to that which exists between two friends or between husband and wife, the kind of personal relationship which we look for in a home. But there is another form of relationship which seems equally important for the expression and development of personal being, and that is the kind of associative relationship which is to be found in a community of work. Where people combine in a common enterprise which is of value and concern to them all, they discover a fulfilment of certain aspects of their personal being which are not fulfilled in any other way. Personal being, then, seems to call for the pursuit of a common aim as well as the acceptance of others as beings with individualities and interests of their own.

Now what can be said of personal relationships at the human level may also have some application to the relationship between man and God. This relationship, too, is, at its most profound, one both of confrontation and of co-operation. The question of the proper structure of the divine-human relationship is discussed in an interesting and provocative way in Harvey Cox's book *The Secular City*. He writes: 'The tribal relationship is of a *pre*-I-Thou type. The deficient individuation of tribal man prevents his experiencing God as fully "other". Not only does he find God in a

[8] T. R. Milford, *Foolishness to the Greeks*, London 1953, p. 86.

horizontal way, but he is always a part of God and vice versa. Man *participates* in God. In a society marked by *vertical* authority, the period of culture and individualism, man tends to experience God in the classic I-Thou encounter. God is seen as another who has authority *over* me. The relationship is one of confrontation. We have suggested earlier that a new type of interhuman relationship seems to be emerging in urban society, one that is just as human as I-Thou but is qualitatively different. It occurs often in the kind of work team described above, a relationship one has in addition to I-Thou experiences in the family and with intimate friends. But it is more significant and very different from the I-It relationship. Rather than participation or confrontation, it is a relationship of *alongsidedness*.'[9] Participation, confrontation, alongsidedness—or what I have called co-operation. Whereas Cox suggests that these are alternative ways of conceiving the divine-human relationship, I would argue that they are descriptions of three permanent and inter-connected aspects of this relationship. They all have a place in the expression and development of fully personal being. There is a sense, as we have already urged, in which participation may be interpreted in a personal rather than an impersonal way, when it implies no absorption or loss of the part in the whole, but an interpenetration of personal being, without the loss of individuality. Again, confrontation itself may be seen as a permanent pole of personal being, complementary to alongsidedness, and not superseded by it. A person needs to know that he is an individual whose being is not exhausted in the roles he plays in society, and it is in face-to-face relationships of friendship and love—relationships of mutual regard and respect rather than relationships, as Cox suggests, of hierarchical authority—that he is reassured of his individuality. He is regarded for what he is in himself more obviously than for what he can do. It is his company which is valued rather than his competence. It must be added, however, that it is in the sharing of common pursuits, in doing things together, that companionship more often than not finds its expression.

The purpose of this digression has been to suggest that an analysis

[9] Harvey E. Cox, *The Secular City*, London and New York 1965, p. 263.

of personal being in human terms may itself lend support to the suggestion that an interpretation of man's communion with God in personal categories will make room for both the element of confrontation and the element of co-operation. The believer will live before God and towards God on the one hand, with God in the world on the other. His participation in the divine life will revolve around both these poles. The movement of reconciliation will be both vertical and horizontal. Consequently we shall expect to find in the practice of prayer, in man's communion with God, a deepening both of his confrontation with God and of his co-operation with him. And this is precisely what we do find—on the one hand thanksgiving, praise and penitence, on the other intercession and petition.

Let us consider first of all man's existence before God, his confrontation with God, in which an apprehension of the being of God is combined with a new understanding of himself. In particular, let us concentrate on the prayer of penitence and the experience of forgiveness. We find that this apprehension is one of being made whole, one of liberation from the forces which have alienated man from the sources of his own true being, one of the forgiveness of sin. The Pharisees rightly perceived that God and only God could forgive sin, since sin is nothing less than alienation, not only from oneself, nor even from one's neighbour, but also from the ultimate ground of all being, alienation from God. The sinner apprehends the forgiveness of his sins as the act of God, partly because he receives this forgiveness—that is, the restoration of his personal being is not within the compass of his own will to bring about, it is something that happens to him rather than something that he himself does—but also because it brings with it, at least in principle, a new understanding of life as a whole. It has 'cosmic' significance. The world is seen in a new light as the object of God's creative and redemptive care. Men are seen as creatures whom God loves. Indeed their forgiveness is implicitly contained within his own. 'If you do not forgive others, then the wrongs you have done will not be forgiven by your Father.'[10] In the experience

[10] Matthew 6.15 (NEB).

of forgiveness the particular and the universal are conjoined.

It is to the experience of the forgiveness of sin that many believers would point if pressed to justify their talk of the personal activity of God. Here, they would say, if anywhere, we have reason to speak of God's activity *in* the world and to use the language of personal relations. A central feature in the case for accepting the life and person of Jesus Christ as the pattern of God's activity in the world is the fact that by his words and actions he mediated forgiveness to others. 'If Christ's humanity is to be seen in the fact that He is tempted and alone, His divinity is to be seen in His offering man the forgiveness of God.'[11] This forgiveness is felt to be neither a violation of man's freedom nor a condonation of his sin. It is in fact a forgiveness of the sinner rather than of the sin. The sinner is restored to a gracious relationship with God. Sinner though he is, he is now a *forgiven* sinner.

It may be asked whether we are right to attribute this forgiveness of sins to an 'act' of God. For instance, W. G. Maclagan argues that a close consideration of the prayer for forgiveness reveals that the concept of God's activity implicit in the language of this prayer is 'not the unambiguously personal concept that the language of petition suggests'. His main contention is that forgiveness is an attitude rather than an act. 'To forgive is essentially to be in a certain state of mind. . . . There is here no *act* of forgiving at all, in the ordinary sense of "act". Any specific act is not itself the forgiving but the means of conveying to the person forgiven the consciousness that he is forgiven already. The consciousness of forgiveness is, correspondingly, the consciousness of being the object of this unresentful love.' Professor Maclagan concludes from this, first, 'that the prayer for forgiveness . . . must be understood to be something other than the petition that it appears to be—an asking God to change His attitude and action towards us, as though He were not already perfect in love', and, secondly, that the prayer for forgiveness must therefore be interpreted as an expression of penitence rather than petition for forgiveness—'what we have is not penitence *and* petition, but rather penitence expressed *as* petition; and it is by

---

[11] G. Wingren, *Gospel and Church*, p. 80.

penitence and not by petition that the achievement of the right relationship is conditioned, by a change wrought in us and not by a
change wrought in God.'[12] With the general tenor of Professor
Maclagan's remarks we may agree. The petition for forgiveness is
not an attempt to change God's mind. It is itself made in the confidence that God is perfect love, and that there is no question about
his will to forgive. It is also the case that prayer for forgiveness can
properly be made only in a spirit of penitence, and to this extent it
may be called an expression of penitence. Even so, I am not sure
that it is correct to eliminate all petitionary element from the prayer
for forgiveness and to discern no 'special activity' on the part of God.
The penitent is not only voicing his sincere grief and contrition
when he asks for forgiveness; he is also asking for something which
he has no moral right to expect. He is asking for a new, undeserved
expression of the divine love which will restore him to a right relationship. Although in one sense he may be confident of the unchanging love of God, in another sense that is just what he has no *right*
to presume upon. To presume upon love is to blaspheme against
it: *'Dieu pardonnera, car c'est son métier.'* We may put the same
matter in another way. There is no such thing as 'cheap grace'.
God's love is not untouched by human sin. The perfection of his
love is shown in ever-new 'acts' of forgiveness, in which he freely
seeks to restore to communion with himself the sinner who by his
sin has disrupted this communion and injured the divine love. It is
because impersonal language fails to do justice to this side of the
experience of forgiveness, giving rise to the notion that divine forgiveness is automatic—produced by man's penitence rather than
conditioned by it—that the language of human petition and of divine
act must be retained. Professor Maclagan himself writes: 'Forgiving
love . . . does not wait for penitence, nor of course does the penitence in any way earn or pay for the love. The total perfected transaction, then, in which forgiveness—the freely forgiving and being
freely forgiven—is joined with the consciousness of forgiveness,
constitutes or restores, it may be with enrichment, a personal relationship that is essentially a meeting of two loves mediated by peni-

[12] W. G. Maclagan, *The Theological Frontier of Ethics*, London 1961, pp. 158-160.

tence.'[13] The only comment I would wish to add to this description of forgiveness is that in such a 'transaction' the sinner sees the primary action as God's and not his own. It is God who acts in restoring the relationship. Acts rather than attitudes constitute and reconstitute personal relationships.

What begins as confrontation soon moves on to co-operation. Penitence and praise proceed to intercession and petition. The personal activity of God experienced as the forgiveness of sins cannot be restricted to a private I-Thou relationship between God and the individual. As we have already remarked, the renewal of the individual's own being carries with it an impetus towards the renewal of the whole of life. It is not possible to be forgiven by God without forgiving one's fellow men. The commandments to love God and to love one's neighbour are indivisible. There is no limit to the extent of God's love, which is universal. Consequently the will of God is apprehended as a will for the reconciliation of all men to himself and to one another, and the activity of God in the world now presses outwards from the individual to include his neighbour. The believer becomes God's fellow-worker, and is called to participate in the divine ministry of reconciliation. This ministry, in which God himself may be said to be active, since it allows the fuller expression of his will, is a ministry both of prayer and of work. In prayer it is an anticipation of that perfect reconciliation which forms part of the Christian hope. In work it is the movement in the world towards the fulfilment of that hope. In both prayer and work it is the penetration of the human creature by the love of God and the extension through him of the formative power of the divine activity. Thus the human prayer of intercession is a moment in the divine work of salvation. M. Nédoncelle puts this point in an especially striking way in his important book on *The Nature and Use of Prayer*: 'When we ask God for a man's welfare, we put before God (and ourselves) what is best in that man; or at least we have come to realize the element in him which offers hope for his restoration; we go right back and see him as a child of God issuing from his Creator's hands unblemished. . . . When I pray for my enemy, I

[13] *Op. cit.*, p. 159.

am praying for reconciliation; and when I pray that enemies may
be reconciled, I have already, through God's action, reconciled them
in myself. There is something in them that has achieved harmony,
and this something only exists in me and through me. Nowhere else
as yet has their ultimate condition been reached.'[14] 'Prayer is thus
the springtime of the world, the flowering of that action which
will issue in constructive labour, the seed of renewed institutions.'[15]
The ground and justification of all intercessory prayer is the faith
that the love of God experienced in the forgiveness of sins embraces
all men everywhere and draws them into a unity not only with himself but with each other in a great communion of saints. The forgiven sinner is himself called to participate through prayer and
action in the eternal purposes of the creative love of God.

Since the hoped-for *parousia* includes the resurrection of the body
as well as the communion of saints, the perfection of nature as well as
of the spirit, intercession will recognize no hard and fast differentia-
tion between the natural and the spiritual. The Christian hope is
all-inclusive, and its anticipation in prayer will also be all-inclusive.
Prayer, to quote Nédoncelle again, 'leads us to the realization that
no order of things can be final that is not cosmic in extent. It spurs
us on to a total view of reality.'[16] When, for example, we pray for
the sick, it is their total well-being that we posit, health of body as
well as health of soul. And recollecting that their health is dependent
for its being on many causes and conditions, natural and spiritual,
our prayer extends to include, in principle, the whole web of
creaturely being. There is a movement from the particular to the
universal, for the love of God is neither partial nor limited. At the
same time there is also a movement from the universal to the particular, since the universality of God's love is no general benevolence lacking care and concern for the particular. 'Prayer,' it has
been said, 'is the expansion of worship into the particular.'[17] It is
also the raising of the particular into the context of the universal. In
the love of God for his creatures particular and universal coalesce.

---

[14] M. Nédoncelle, *The Nature and Use of Prayer*, London 1964, p. 118.

[15] *Op. cit.*, p. 119.

[16] *Ibid.*

[17] A. C. Turner, in *Concerning Prayer*, ed., B. H. Streeter, London 1916, p. 444.

So prayer that never includes particularities may lack any profound engagement with the created world, while prayer which never rises above the particular may never find its true centre in God.

We have suggested that Christian prayer is an anticipation of the *parousia,* and we have taken as our pattern of the *parousia* the person of Christ, expressed in his relation to God, to man and to nature. We must, however, beware of professing a greater knowledge than we have any right to claim. 'We are God's children; what we shall be has not yet been disclosed, but we know that when it is disclosed we shall be like him.'[18] Consequently in all prayer there will be a large measure of openness, of adventure. It is not the operation of a technique, it is a response of learning and love. 'Prayer is for the particular; but it deals with things in the spirit of the artist and the discoverer, and not that of the manufacturer.'[19] Although God has revealed himself in the person of Christ, he remains mysterious. Consequently prayer will combine a large measure of agnosticism concerning the details of God's will with a firm confidence in his providence. And since God has chosen through man and with man to complete his creative purposes, calling him to participate in the work of his love, prayer will also be a discipline in which man seeks to learn what is the divine will for him here and now in his present situation. He will hear no inner voice instructing him what to do. He will still be involved in the responsibilities of discovering the relevant facts and of making the necessary decisions. But, for the man of prayer, deliberation and decision will be rooted in reflection on the eternal purposes of God revealed in Christ and nourished by faith in God's secret activity in the believer himself. 'Man knows and acts, but no longer with the activity of his own unassisted nature; he knows and acts personally . . . because he has become as it were bonded to God who enables him to be with him and in him in such a way that, simultaneously, God both operates all things within us and makes us autonomous.'[20]

---

[18] I John 3.2 (NEB).
[19] A. C. Turner, *op. cit.*, p. 407.
[20] M. Nédoncelle, *op. cit.*, p. 154.

It is clear from what we have been saying that we expect prayer to make a difference to the man who prays—just as we should expect to see a difference in a man who stopped to think what he was doing, or in a man who fell in love. We have argued that there is a very proper sense in which we may speak of the activity of God engaging and eliciting a response of love and obedience in the depths of the human spirit. In communion with God a man comes to a new knowledge of himself and a new apprehension of the world around him. We have seen that this communion cannot be restricted to a private relationship between God and the individual, but moves towards a total vision of all things in harmonious response to God in fulfilment of the divine will and purpose, and issues in action which seeks to embody and express that will in the actual imperfect situation in which the individual finds himself. Thus we may speak of God's acting in the world through the response of the faithful. His activity in the world is mediated through man; it is, as it were, an indirect activity rather than a direct activity. For a faith which has its source in the belief that it was in and through a man that God wrought the salvation of the world, it is nothing surprising that the norm for our interpretation of God's response to prayer is to be found in his indwelling in human hearts and minds and his inspiration of human thought and action. Is this, however, the full measure of God's response? Does he answer our prayers only by helping us to help ourselves? Can he ever be said to do for us in the world what we cannot do for ourselves? The concerted witness of countless Christian believers reveals a conviction that God does just this, that there are in fact occasions when he answers prayer directly by granting what is asked. What are we to say in view of such a persistent belief?

Several objections even to the serious consideration of such a suggestion at once arise, objections which lie near the surface of our whole discussion and which emerge sharply just at this point.

First, it may be said that the whole idea of God's answering prayer by some special action in the world betrays an anthropomorphic and naturalistic concept of God, whose being is transcendent of this world and whose activity, if activity is the right word at all, is universal. To this we may reply that our use of the language of personal being in speaking of God, for which we have tried to give some justification, is bound to be anthropomorphic to some extent, simply because personal being is known to us through the exercise of it ourselves. With Lotze, however, we may hold that personal being is not necessarily limited being; and when we ascribe it to God we negate those limitations which are associated with it in our own human experiences. Thus, for example, when we pray to God for some particular benefit, there is no question of our informing God of certain things of which he was ignorant or forgetful, as if we were reminding an absent-minded professor that he was expected to be at a particular place to give a lecture which he had promised to deliver. 'Your heavenly Father knoweth that ye have need of all these things.'[21] In St Augustine's words: 'God does not ask us to tell him our needs in order that he may learn about them, but in order that we may be made capable of receiving his gifts.'[22] Nor is there any question of our persuading God to do some good simply because we ask for it, despite the apparent implications of the parable of the importunate widow. If God is good, he does not need to be prompted and prodded to act in accordance with his goodness. In reply to the comment that if God were good he would not wait to be asked before doing what was for the best we should have to affirm, first, that he does not 'wait', in the sense of doing nothing, for his activity is unceasing and his grace is prevenient; but, second, that the fulfilment of his purpose may itself be conditional upon our approaching him in prayer and what is ultimately for the best itself dependent upon our praying. Quite clearly such an affirmation would owe more to an underlying and persistent trust in the wisdom and goodness of God than to any straightforward assessment of the empirical facts. We are here confronted with one more of the many facets of the problem of evil, and, as on other occasions, faith takes on the character of a defiant 'nevertheless'. The grounds for its persistence in the face of the empirical facts must be sought elsewhere. Lastly, to the objection that God's activity is transcendent and universal we should answer that, true

[21] Matthew 6.32.   [22] St Augustine, *To Proba*, VIII, 17.

as this undoubtedly is, it does not preclude our speaking also of his particular activity, through which there is a fuller expression of his will and extension of his purpose. When we speak of God in terms of personal being, the universal and particular are not exclusive concepts.

Second, it may be said that the scientific view of the order of the world prevents our taking seriously the suggestion that an event in the world may be 'caused' by the immediate volition of God. To this far-reaching objection we shall content ourselves with a brief reply. If the scientific view of the order of the world can make room for human freedom and human volition without disrupting its own procedures, so too can it, in principle, make room for divine freedom and divine volition; for although it is impossible for us to know what the relation of God to the world is in itself or the way in which it is dependent upon his creative will, it is the relation of the human will to human behaviour that we look to for an analogy. Admittedly, this too is difficult to fathom, and various analyses of it are possible. But here we must be allowed to assume without argument that in certain circumstances men have the power to transcend their past and to initiate actions for which no impersonal account can provide a complete explanation, however many and varied causal stories it may be possible and appropriate to tell, since even free human actions are embedded in the natural order and participate in it. Similarly, the divine creativity may be said to operate within the natural order without disrupting it. There will, in that case, be no 'miraculous intervention', but simply a *'concursus dei'*.[23] (If it is allowed that the natural order as we know it is only relative, and that it is possible for it to be subsumed under a higher and as yet unknown order, then we may find a place also for the idea of God's miraculous activity in the world without involving him to a charge of arbitrary intervention.)[24]

[23] See Barth, *Church Dogmatics III*, 3, Edinburgh 1961, pp. 94f.; and H. Gollwitzer, *The Existence of God*, pp. 55f.

[24] An adequate analysis of the concept of miracle will include *both* a religious aspect in which an event is seen as the expression of the loving activity of God *and* also a non-religious aspect in which it is inexplicable in terms of the known laws of nature.

H

The third, and from the religious angle probably the most telling, objection is a moral one, what we may call the problem of distribution in the pattern of answered prayer. Suppose we allow that God acts directly in the world in answer to prayer. Can we, however, discern any coherent moral and spiritual pattern linking the occasions on which he grants a petition with those on which he refuses? Do we really see the working together of all things for good in both groups of occasions? Is it not more likely that what appear to be answers to our prayers are coincidental occurrences which would have happened anyhow, whether we had prayed or not? Are we convinced that God has good reason for granting in one instance what he refuses in another? There are few, I suspect, who would claim to see such rhyme and reason. They might do their best to distinguish between the different instances so as to account for God's differing responses. They might say that certain petitions were too trivial for God to grant,[25] or that the supplicant had not sufficient faith and that because of this lack of faith God withheld his hand. But in the end they are likely simply to reassert their conviction that there must be such a pattern issuing from the divine wisdom in spite of their failure actually to discern it. God *is* a God who answers prayer when it accords with his wisdom and will, although we have to confess that we cannot fathom the depths of his wisdom or penetrate the mystery of his will.

We seem to have reached something of an impasse, but perhaps we shall be able to make a little further progress if we ask ourselves what would count for the believer as an answer to his prayer, and in what way he would justify his conviction that God does answer prayer.

Suppose that I pray for something to happen, and it does not happen. I might then say that God had *not* granted my petition. If asked to give some explanation why he had not granted it, I might go on to say that the object of my petition was not what he himself willed. If what I asked him for seemed on the face of it utterly unselfish and in every way desirable, and so on moral grounds to be the sort of thing that one would judge to be in accord with the will

<hr />

[25] Cf. H. D. Lewis, *Our Experience of God*, London 1959, Chapter XVII.

of God, I might add that in the conditions prevailing at that time it was not possible for God to grant my request. To the retort that all things are possible for God, I should have to reply that, although there might be some sense in which this was true, there is another sense in which it is not true. God's being and purposes together rule out certain things which, when considered abstractly, might be thought possible. If I then go on to claim that God had in a way answered my prayer by refusing to grant my petition, I am not necessarily wriggling out of a difficulty, but I am saying that in and through his refusal I have apprehended something more of his presence and activity. The answer in this case is in terms of a deeper religious awareness, of a growth in a personal relationship with God. The affirmation that God answers prayer is here a religious affirmation grounded in the apprehension of a relationship with God in which the language of dialogue, of address and answer, is felt to be appropriate. The corollary to be drawn from this observation is that, to the extent that the whole of life is interpreted as a dialogue with God, all events may be seen as expressing the divine answer. On the other hand, if we are prepared to use the language of purpose in respect of God's activity, and to say that he is working within the limiting conditions of his own creation, then some of God's answers will be, as it were, more reluctant than others, less expressive of his complete and perfect will. An answer of this sort may be the frightening silence of God.

Suppose, on the other hand, that what I pray for does happen. I might then say that God *had* granted my petition. Should I mean anything more by this than that God had answered my prayer in the same sense as he could be said to have answered my prayer when what I prayed for did not happen—namely, that through this particular occurrence I had attained a deeper awareness of the over-all love and providence of God? I am inclined to say that I should mean something more, namely, that my prayer was in some way instrumental in bringing about this occurrence, that had I not prayed as I did what happened would not have happened. The empirical evidence for such a belief is, as I have said before, not obviously favourable. But we are not treating petition and answer in any mechanical way; we are setting the prayer in the context of a relationship between man and God which is all-embracing, and we are affirming that within the particularity of this context, at this particular juncture of events here and now, this particular prayer is a significant factor in shaping what follows after. It is not a magical formula. It is a moment in the total response of the human creature to his creator, a moment which, perhaps, removes a condition restricting the fuller expression of the divine will. The occurrence is thus seen as an instance of God's providential activity, a sign of the furthering of his purposes.

No doubt the believer's own experience has a lot to do with the question whether he does or does not believe that God answers prayer in this way. It will strengthen or weaken his belief, it will count for or against his conviction. He may think there is sufficient evidence to suggest that ordinary physical causes are not the only causes which operate in the natural world. He may appeal to the evidence of telepathy and psycho-kinesis to support his case. But when all is said and done, the real ground for his conviction will lie elsewhere, namely, in what he believes to be the character of God and the relation of God to the world. The question at issue is this: is God such that we should expect him to answer prayer in this way? In coming to grips with this question the believer takes as his norm the insights associated with the person of Christ.

Obstacles of all sorts, not least his own preconceptions, condition what he sees. Consequently no straightforward or simple appeal to the pattern and example of Christ, or to the nature of Christian experience derived from him, is possible. However, the argument might run on the following lines.

The whole tenor of Christ's teaching supports the use of personal language to describe man's relationship with God. God is Father. He calls his children into a relationship of obedience and trust. It is this relationship which is prime importance; everything else is subordinate. However, although this relationship is essentially personal, it is not narrowly spiritual. God is not only Father, he is also Lord. The whole world is his: he is King. Nature and history both come under his rule. Nevertheless, his rule is not yet fully exercised. The world is 'in the power of the evil one'. Man must look forward to a future when God's rule will be open and not hidden. In the meantime God's rule is exercised through those who respond to his love and co-operate in his purposes. To them belongs a present responsibility and a future joy. Thus God's providence is both universal and particular. Because he is Lord, his active care is universal. Because he is Father, it is also particular. It is known by man especially in the forgiveness of his sins and his restoration to a right relationship with his God. But the spiritual is not divorced from the material: 'Set your mind on God's kingdom and his justice before everything else, and all the rest will come to you as well.'[26] Thus God is active in his world, concerned with the spiritual and the material, the general and the particular.

In Christ's own response to God we discern two aspects. On the one hand, there is his acceptance of the limitation of the natural order. He is involved in the conditions of the world. He accepts its sufferings. In temptations he rejects the whole notion of invoking supernatural powers. Obedience to his Father's will leads him along the way of the cross. There is no escaping the agony and the pain. On the other hand, there streams through him the power of divine love. He heals the sick, he stills the storm. We may not know where to draw the line between the factual and the symbolic, but we are gripped with the sense that the achievements of Christ in obedient response to the love of God shatter our conceptions of what is natural and possible. 'If Christ ever came to His disciples walking on the water, it was because love demanded it, and not in virtue of a mysterious power to command at will the physical forces of nature. Even if He did so, it would be nearer the truth to disbelieve it than to believe it because of any other reason than that of love. Even if He did not, it might be nearer the truth to believe that He might have done so, because of love, than to disbelieve the possibility because of science. Had men the love of Christ, they would also know of His power.'[27]

It is time to bring these tentative remarks to a conclusion. Perhaps it is a mistake to think of God's doing something in response

---

[26] Matthew 6.33 (NEB). [27] A. C. Turner, *op. cit.*, p. 402.

to our prayer, as if our prayer had persuaded God to do what he could have done but refused to do without our praying for it. Perhaps we ought rather to think that our asking in faith may make it possible for God to do something which he could not have done without our asking. We may give the divine Love a *point d'appui*, so that through our prayer it may realize possibilities which only in this way it can actualize. Perhaps we must go on praying in the faith and hope that this is so, even though we cannot yet explain how it is so. In prayer we refuse to accept as ultimate what appear to be the fixed conditions of the world, because we believe that these conditions are not ultimate. They have a temporary validity within the purpose of God, but they are in the end subordinate to his love. We do not yet know what love can or cannot achieve. Our faith prompts us to pray, in Kierkegaard's phrase, even 'for the impossible'. Prayer 'is a form of expectation'.[28] It is the growing point in the divine-human encounter. It is participation in new creation.

[28] M. Nédoncelle, *op. cit.*, p. 81.

VI

The Faithfulness of God

CHRISTIAN belief in the providential activity of God is a faith in his universal lordship over the whole of his creation. It is the affirmation not only of the goodness of his original creative purposes—so much might be affirmed by a deism which posited an architect and designer of the world—but of the continuation of his creative work and the furtherance of his purposes within creation. His activity is both transcendent and immanent. Nothing is concealed from his presence, nothing is untouched by his love. He is the origin and the goal of the universe, its alpha and its omega. His love sustains the world as it is and draws it towards that perfection which it has in it to attain.

The believer does not derive this faith from some purely objective consideration of the way the world of his ordinary experience goes. He sees signs of the divine activity and providence in the world, and these support his faith. But the evidence which these afford does not of itself necessitate it. They do not of themselves constitute the basis for a compelling inference to the activity of God. They become signs of his activity only when combined with a prior non-inferential apprehension of God. Because of the radical imperfection and the apparent indifference of the world the believer has at times to assert his faith against the appearances. The appearances as such are ambiguous. Faith recognizes this ambiguity. Hence it remains faith. But it renders an account of itself. It has its reasons and presents its evidence. It does not lack a case.

The distinctive character of Christian faith derives from an apprehension of God mediated through the life and person of Jesus Christ. It is he who gives this apprehension its clarity and its content. He is the sign of signs. 'It is not the case that the man who believes in providence may easily or by means of any art read the book of history and see there the ways of providence. It is the case, however, that the Word of God in which he believes, and which he believes, can as such cause him to see something of God's rule, not His universal plan or total view, but God Himself at work at various points, and always and in every respect enough to give the man's faith in Him the character of a knowledge in which he may genuinely and rightly live by his faith.'[1]

Expressed in the first instance existentially as the forgiveness of sins, the gift of self-understanding and the renewal of personal life, this apprehension also contains within itself a new vision both of history and of nature. The existential insight is of cosmic significance. It is a religious insight precisely because it binds together the personal and the universal.

Thus the forgiveness of sins looks forward to a transformation of personal life and its worldly conditions. The new life of the spirit is a foretaste of future glory, when the Love reflected in the reconciliation of the sinner also will transfigure the world. The providence of God presses towards this consummation which is beyond our comprehension, but which is implicit in the faith evoked through Christ, the pattern of whose life faith sees as the pattern of God's purposes and activity.

In prayer the believer holds before him this future hope. His communion with God is already an anticipation of what is still to be revealed, a confession of the transcendent and transforming power of the divine love.

The obvious danger inherent in this approach to an understanding of providence and prayer, with its insistence on the future triumph of love and on its present anticipation, of transformation and transfiguration, is that it evades the harsh realities of the temporal process—its pain and struggle, its tragedy and inconclusiveness. It may

---

[1] K. Barth, *Church Dogmatics.* III, 3. p. 24.

be argued that these are the very characteristics which constituted the spring-board for the religious instinct and prepared the way for an initial apprehension, through them but in contrast to them, of the complete, the perfect and the abiding. But a true religion dare not ignore these temporal realities and dismiss them as mere appearances. The charge which we levelled against all attempts to see the world as a rational or moral unity was that they foundered on the realities of human freedom and of non-moral as well as moral evil. Because of these realities we sought the unity and perfection of the world not in the world itself but in the transcendent will of God, and we suggested that the purposes of God themselves demanded a universe in a measure independent of him, in which his love had to seek an entry which by its very nature it could not compel. Unwilling to abandon the whole notion of the working out of God's purposes in creation, we have suggested that his own creation places certain limitations on his activity, and we now find ourselves facing the question whether God can indeed be limited in this way and still remain God.

What, for example, are we to say about the ultimacy and omnipotence of God? If the processes of nature and history are a real becoming, if our human choices are originating factors in these processes, in what sense can God still be said to be ultimate and omnipotent? Has he not abrogated his sovereignty and descended from his throne? In letting the world go, so to speak, in order to give it that measure of independence which will allow it to be something and man to be someone, has he not let it slip out of his grasp altogether? If God respects man's freedom, and waits upon his prayers and works together with him in the world, then he himself is surely involved in change and in a real sense dependent upon man for the achievement of his purposes. His activity in the world is matched by a certain passivity. But if all this is so, is God still God, perfect being, beyond the vagaries of change and chance? Or has he become one of us? We may still love him, but can we still completely trust him? He will, no doubt, do his best, but is his best good enough?

There have been many proposals at different times to speak of a limited God, whose limitations arise from the manner of his involvement in the world. Always, however, they have met with the religious comment, that such a God could not evoke that obedient worship and unreserved commitment which are characteristic of the religious response.[2] This has, indeed, been questioned. But the general consensus of religious writings seems to favour the view that the complete self-surrender demanded of the believer is appropriate only if God is all-powerful as well as all-good.

There have been various classical attempts to combine belief in human freedom with belief in the omnipotence of God. For example, it has been argued that in his single and indivisible creative activity God foresees and predetermines the whole spatio-temporal process. Of course the language of fore-seeing and fore-determining is itself misleading, as God is said to be 'outside' the temporal process. There is no before and after in the divine activity; it is single, indivisible and timeless. I must confess that I find it extremely difficult to make sense of the notion of a timeless activity. However, leaving this difficulty for the moment on one side, let us look at the implicit suggestion that past, present and future are equally open to God in an eternal present. A spatial analogy is often pressed into service to render this suggestion more plausible. A good example of this may be found in Thomas Traherne's *Felicities*: 'Eternity is a Mysterious Absence of Times and Ages: an Endless Length of Ages always present, and for ever perfect. For as there is an immovable Space wherein all finite Spaces are enclosed, and all Motions carried on and performed; so is there an Immovable Duration, that contains and measures all moving Durations. . . . We pass through a Standing Continent or Region of Ages, that are already before us, glorious and perfect while we come to them.'[3] So God knows our choices, our sins, our prayers from all eternity, and from all eternity he has met them with his grace and providence. But what are we to make of this line of argument? Is not the spatial

---

[2] See, for example, D. M. Baillie's sensitive discussion of this point in *Faith in God*, London 1964, Chapter VIII. Also James Richmond, 'God, Time and Philosophy', *Theology*, May 1965, pp. 234ff.

[3] *Felicities of Thomas Traherne*, ed. Sir Arthur Quiller-Couch, London 1934, pp. 105f.

analogy fundamentally deceptive? Certainly we may take in more or less objects at a single glance, and allow our eyes to run from one to the other, backwards and forwards. But have we any experience of taking in even a part of the future, as we have of the present and past? Is the future merely the as yet unfolded roll of time? Does it, in any real sense, already exist? If it is asserted that it does already exist, and that on occasions we do have immediate access to it, as for example in cases of precognition, then it may perhaps be said that God always has immediate access to it. It may also be argued that the proposition that God already knows what choices we shall make does not entail the proposition that God pre-determines our choices; that consequently it is logically possible for man to make his choices freely, but for God so to have determined the order of the world that the outcome of these choices will fit in with his own over-riding purposes. As against this, however, we must ask in what sense God could be said to know our choices before we made them? I can say to John that I know which chocolate he is going to choose before he chooses it, but this is no more than a highly probable guess on the basis of past experience. I am not immediately aware of his as yet future act of choosing; and he may confound my claim to knowledge by deliberately choosing a different kind from usual. Perhaps the only occasion when I might claim to know with certainly what another person would do at some moment in the future would be one on which I myself had pre-determined his action, through hypnotism or some other means of suggestion. But then we should hesitate to say that this action was the outcome of the person's own choice. On this analogy, if God were said to know my decisions before I made them, it would be because he had in some way engineered my decisions, so that they were no longer really mine but his!

I do not wish to argue that there is no conceivable sense in which God may be said to know our decisions before we know them ourselves. To him 'all hearts are open, all desires known', and from him 'no secrets are hid'. However, human analogies are here of little help. Presumably, such divine knowledge would in no way resemble our own discursive predictions of the future. God does not work out future probabilities on the basis of past experience. Furthermore, the notion of a kind of divinely intuitive knowledge of the future is implausible. It is tied too closely to spatial analogies, while the future is not of the same logical status as the past. The past, we say, is fixed, but the future is open. The content of our decisions does not exist until we have made them. Our decisions are in our own power. If we take the claims of human freedom seriously, and interpret it as the ability in some ways to transcend ourselves and even to make ourselves—difficult as these ideas obviously are—then we shall have also to take the fact of temporality seriously, and refuse to concede that it can be simply embraced within a timeless eternity. We may say that God is com-present with us in our decisions. He does not have to wait to discover how we have decided. But these decisions are not already made in some timeless eternity.

If we allow that the world-process is not completely determined and that it contains, at least at the human level, an element of creative novelty, we must ask ourselves what this admission involves for our understanding of the providential activity of God. In what sense can he still be said to exercise a universal lordship?

In the first place, we may see the exercise of a general providence in the restrictions placed upon indeterminacy. No world can be completely indeterminate if it is to be a world. There must be some order if there is to be a development of things and persons with a relative stability and persistence within the processes of change. So we may say that God's general control is to be seen in the properties which belong to the fundamental constituent particles which in their developing inter-relations have made the world what it is. It is conceivable that these properties might have been other than they are, that they might never have produced the world of organic and then of personal and rational life.

It may further be claimed that these same properties place certain general limits on the random effects of indeterminacy, that there is an over-all movement towards harmony and co-ordination. Now this notion may indeed be of some use when we are seeking for God's providential control of nature, but it is not so immediately plausible when we attempt to apply it to human history. Ideas of automatic progress, whether evolutionary or dialectical, have no longer the appeal that once they had. There are destructive forces within the human spirit which have in the twentieth century erupted and shattered Western European man's earlier easy optimism. On the other hand, it may be said that there are factors even in the human condition which urge man in the direction of justice and peace. If he is to survive at all, he must learn to exercise a common humanity.

A further difficulty, however, in such a conception of God's providence lies in the fact that it is so general. What of the countless ill-starred and unfortunate by-products of this over-all purpose? The suggestion that God exercises a general control over all things is of little comfort to the man who finds himself the product of one of nature's less successful experiments. The notion of God's general providence threatens to become a blasphemous mockery if it is this and nothing more. God sacrifices the individual on the altar of his cosmic plan. It does not matter how many perish so long as the last battle is won. And yet what more is there to be said if God has created the world with a constitution which functions in just this way? It is no wonder that there are those who deny the traditional doctrine of creation and who see the activity of God manifested solely in a rescue-operation from a fundamentally alien and hostile Nature.

If we refuse to accept this complete divorce of Nature and God, we cannot avoid making some appeal to this notion of God's *general* providence. We must certainly allow for something like a divine indiscriminacy. A trusting to providence, in the sense of leaving the future to look after itself, is not the sum-total of a Christian counsel of perfection. Nor is the invocation of Providence a substitute for the responsible exercise of human wisdom and choice. Nevertheless, we must interpret the divine indiscriminacy itself as a sign of divine benevolence. Jesus' saying that God 'makes his sun rise on good and bad alike, and sends the rain on the honest and dishonest'[4] is to be interpreted as an illustration drawn from the indiscriminacy of the processes of nature and applied to the indis-

[4] Matthew 5.45 (NEB).

criminacy of the universal love of God. But rain and sunshine sometimes become storm and drought. These too are part of that indiscriminacy of nature which is a condition for the development of human rationality and responsibility. Consequently these too, though in a roundabout way, are to be interpreted as a sign of the benevolence of God.

God's benevolence and general providence are, religiously speaking, still inadequate. In fact for the believer there can be no satisfaction with a general providence which is not also a special providence. His own existential needs raise the specifically religious question, and a satisfying religious answer must meet those needs. That is, the providence of God must be such as to extend to the individual in his particular situation.

Now we have noted that at the heart of the religious response is the sense of the forgiveness of sin. God reconciles a man to himself, he establishes him in a new and saving relationship. It could, then, be argued that God is concerned only with the inwardness of human life, with the cultivation of a man's fundamental attitudes and dispositions, more particularly with the purity of his heart and his obedience to the divine will. The world becomes the scene of soul-making, a religious combat-course. Troubles are sent to try us, but the special providence of God is shown in his enabling the believer to endure the struggle and to overcome the temptation to defect.

The training of character is a pursuit dear to many an English heart, and it would be foolish to deny that the best in life is often achieved only with effort and perseverance. A certain self-mastery and independence of the environment, a recognition that the good things of life fall short of the values of personal affection and love— these are without doubt highly desirable characteristics which can be acquired only in the rough and tumble of life, and the believer will see them as graces given to him by God. So Paul writes: 'I have learned to find resources in myself whatever my circumstances. I know what it is to be brought low, and I know what it is to have plenty. I have been thoroughly initiated into the human lot with all its ups and downs—fullness and hunger, plenty and want. I have strength for anything through him who gives me power.'[5]

But does God care only for a man's character, and is he always testing our endurance? If this were the case, one would have expected at the very least that the tests would be more obviously proportioned to a man's attainments. To appeal at this juncture simply to the sufficiency of God's grace is as little an answer as to appeal to the sufficiency of man's own will-power. Character depends upon physical and mental conditions as well as upon deliberate efforts of the will. In our own providential care for one another we do not merely exhort and encourage, we seek to ameliorate the total conditions of a person's life. We are concerned with a person's complete well-being, and this is conditioned by a whole array of factors outside his control. We desire his happiness and not only his moral goodness. Even Kant, who believed that there was nothing intrinsically good except the good will, admitted that happiness was a constituent factor in the perfect good. In fact one of the special functions of his God was to apportion happiness to desert and so to redress the obvious imparities of this world.

If we are not content to limit God's care and concern to the stiffening of man's moral fibre, but believe that it extends to every aspect of human life; if, that is, we believe that God's very concern for the deepening and developing of a divine human relationship embraces man's whole person in his total embodiment in the world, what can we say about his special providential love for his individual human creatures? Are we restricted to an appeal to his general benevolence and an affirmation that this general benevolence is ultimately served by a particular indiscriminacy? We may be prepared—in fact I would urge that we must be prepared—to argue along these lines. If, however, there is nothing more to be said than this, then the believer's faith that he himself, in whatever situation he finds himself, is under the loving protection of a heavenly father is little short of self-deception. Earthly fathers know how to do better than this for their children!

One of the severest temptations which comes to the man who trusts in the providence of God is the temptation to think that in

[5] Philippians 4.11-13 (NEB).

his time of real need God has abandoned him—that he is a distant God, or an absent God, who does not really care for his creatures, but sports with them as the President of the Immortals sported with Tess. When he has tired of his sport, he tosses them aside to be destroyed. His trust, however, may perhaps be sustained if he can reassure himself of two things—first, that God has not in fact abandoned him; and, second, that although his plight may, humanly speaking, be hopeless, God can deliver him from ultimate despair. To be without God and without hope in the world is to be in the power of the evil one. It is from this living death that Jesus taught his disciples to pray for deliverance.

But God is not absent. Faith proclaims that he is present, present in the first place in his compassion. He has not abandoned his world. He himself is involved in its pain and tragedy. He is not, like some divine Gallio, 'left unconcerned'.[6] He is alongside his creation, sharing both its joys and sorrows. Bonhoeffer's celebrated, if cryptic, words are the most striking expression of this faith that I know, and perhaps I may be forgiven if I quote them once again:

The God who is with us is the God who forsakes us (Mark 15.34). The God who lets us live in the world without the working hypothesis of God is the God before whom we stand continually. *Before God and with God we live without God.* God lets himself be pushed out of the world on to the cross. . . . Only the suffering God can help.[7]

It is of the utmost importance that we give full weight to each phrase in the sentence that I have italicized. The question might well be asked: what is the difference between 'living without God' and having no God at all? Indeed one line of development from Bonhoeffer's remarks has led to the substitution of a religious anthropology for theology, of atheism for theism. But Bonhoeffer's 'living without God' must be understood in the light of his living 'before God and with God'. God still confronts us and challenges us. He still pursues his purposes in the world and calls us to be his fellow-workers. But the structures of the world are a part of his purpose.

[6] Acts 18.17 (NEB).
[7] D. Bonhoeffer, *Letters and Papers from Prison*, pp. 196f.

Their limitations reflect the shaping of his purpose, and their poten-
tialities the hope of its fruition. God is, in Whitehead's phrase, 'the
great companion, the fellow-sufferer who understands'. But he is
more than this. In fact, he is this *because* he is more than this. He
is man's fellow-sufferer because he is also man's God. His compassion is an expression of his providence. His power is the power
of love. His companionship is the companionship of *creative*
love.

Because God is more than a fellow-sufferer he can recreate hope.
But hope for what? We have already seen that there is a subtle
dialectic of rebellion and acceptance in the Christian response to
suffering and evil, and that there is a time and place for both. Something similar must be said about the nature of Christian hope. It
stems from faith in the transfiguring power of the divine love. Love
not only suffers, but also transfigures. So the Christian believer will
look to God to 'bring a happy issue' out of present afflictions. In the
first instance he will hope for such an issue in this life. Nor will
he lightly abandon such a hope, especially where experience has
taught him that the prayer of love can and does work wonders. But
when conditions refuse to yield and he can no longer hope in this
life, his hope will reach out beyond this life. In God nothing will be
lost that can be saved. In unremitting adversity the believer adheres
to the compassion of the divine love in this life and to the transfiguring power of the divine love in the life to come. The logic of
his hope in God's future enables him to face death itself without
despair. The last enemy loses its power to destroy the human spirit,
not because it is accepted as natural and inevitable, but because it is
denied the last word. The last word lies with God. It is a creative
and re-creative word.

We have said that the Christian hope which reaches out beyond
this life is the hope that in God nothing will be lost that can be
saved. Some theologians have interpreted this hope in the sense that
all finite experiences contribute to the divine experience. All that is
of value in human experience is eternal by virtue of becoming part
of the divine experience. In fact human experience can enhance
and enrich the life of God. When we lose ourselves in the love of

I

God, nothing is lost. We perish, but God abides, and in him our eternity is assured.

This is at first sight an attractive view. It encourages us to surrender ourselves to God in confidence that he will conserve all that we ourselves have valued. It by-passes all the difficulties concerning personal identity and the nature of the spiritual body in which the traditional view of resurrection is involved. It is better suited to the whole climate of modern thought. Nevertheless, is it true to say that nothing is lost? Are we anxious to conserve only the valuable experiences as such, considered in abstraction from the person whose experiences they are? If a person is to be identified only with a collection of experiences, then that person may achieve an immortality in God who includes these same experiences in the totality of his own experience. But if we make a distinction between the person who has the experiences and the experiences which he has, so that a person is always something 'more' than his experiences and in some way transcends them; and if we value the person as such, and not only in virtue of his experiences, then something *is* lost. There may here be an immortality of a sort, but it is not personal immortality. There may be no such thing as personal immortality. But personal immortality is what appears to many to be the vital issue at stake. Nor is this view necessarily prompted by hidden motives of selfishness. It is more often of others than of themselves that they are thinking. Hence it is misleading to say that nothing is lost when personal immortality is lost.

The traditional Christian hope of resurrection is centred on the resurrection of Jesus Christ and is the hope that by the spirit of Christ God will raise man to a new order of existence, individual and corporate, in a new world. If a man is no more than a complicated system of physical parts, of which his personal being is only adjectival, then the destruction of the human body is also the destruction of the human person, and there could be no resurrection of the person without the reconstitution of his physical parts. If, however, we are willing to grant that man already possesses a certain creativity and freedom, then we may say that through the development of a highly complex pattern of organic life there has arisen in the world in response to the divine love a being who has a measure of independence of its history and environment, who can to some extent transcend his past and determine his future. Although he is fashioned and conditioned by his past, he is as a person not simply what the past has made him, he can himself transcend it and has the power to shape the conditions which bear upon his future.

Applying these considerations to the person of Christ we may hazard the suggestion that, entering upon the conditions determined by his heritage and heredity, Jesus fashioned them into a life which reflected and embodied the divine love. In his obedience to the divine will he transcended the human condition which he shared with his fellow men, entering upon the freedom of a true humanity, completed and consummated in this final self-surrender to God upon the cross. Death itself was compelled to contribute to life. When God raised Jesus from the dead, it was in one sense his great 'Nevertheless' to the frustrating forces of nature, but in another sense it was the completion of a process which had been taking place throughout Jesus' whole life. It is love which constitutes personal being; it is the same love which raises it from death to life. Love supernaturalizes nature. Out of nature it brings forth personal being. Nature has been the cradle of personal being in the past, and it offers the possibility of the fuller development of personal being in the future. Here we can see the sign of the general providence of God. But something more may be said. At any time and in any place a man may waken to the approach of God, to his call to obedience, to his offer of forgiveness, to his promise of companionship and to his gift of hope. Even death itself may become such a place and such a time, transformed and transfigured into the promise of life, a sign that God's providence is also special and personal.

Thus the cross and the resurrection of Jesus Christ become for Christians the focus of the divine activity. They assure him of God's providence, and they evoke his trust and hope. On the cross they see the compassion of the divine love, God's participation in the tragedy which marks and mars creation. But with the eyes of faith they apprehend through this passivity an activity which is transfiguring the total situation. Evil itself is being compelled to serve a deeper good. Divine and human are becoming at one. 'The Cross of Christ is the Jacob's ladder by which we Ascend into the Highest Heavens. There we see Joyful Patriarchs, Expecting Saints, Prophets Ministering, Apostles Publishing, and Doctors Teaching: all Nations concentering, and Angels Praising. That Cross is a Tree set on fire with invisible flame, that Illuminateth all the World. The flame is Love: the Love in His Bosom who died on it. In the light of which we see how to possess all the Things in Heaven and Earth after His similitude. For He that Suffered on it was the Son of God as you are: tho' He seemed only a Mortal Man. He had Acquaintance and Relations as you have, but He was a Lover of Men and Angels. Was He not the Son of GOD; and Heir of the Whole World? To this poor, Bleeding, Naked Man did all the Corn and Wine, and Oil, and Gold and Silver in the World minister in an Invisible Manner, even as He was exposed Lying and Dying upon the Cross.'[8] The resurrection of Jesus completes and seals the transfiguration which the eye of faith already beholds on the cross. It may or may not be the case that the gospel *pericope* of the transfiguration of Jesus on the mountain was originally a narrative of a post-resurrection appearance. In any case its theological significance is of fundamental importance for understanding the nature of Christian hope. This hope is based on the power of divine love to transfigure, first by accepting the conditions which have been shaped by the past, and second by transforming them into a new being.

We return, then, to what for us must be the final question. The line of argument that we have been pursuing leads to a radical reassessment of the traditional doctrines of the omnipotence and impassibility of God. We have suggested that faith in God's providence is the conviction that his love is doing and will do everything that it can, but that it is in a real sense limited by the conditions of the world and of human freedom. The fact that these limitations are themselves the result of his creative will and are conditions of his creative purpose does not make them any less limiting, although it removes their ultimacy. There is no fate that is more ultimate than

---

[8] T. Traherne, *op. cit.*, pp. 84f.

God himself, and to which he himself is also subject. The conditions themselves derive from the divine will. Even so, if God remains faithful to his own being, revealed in the life, death and resurrection of Jesus Christ, and interpreted as Love, what reason is there for hoping that the conditions which Love itself imposes and observes will not in the end thwart the achievement of Love's own purposes?

As our discussion has developed, we have been led to question the unqualified validity of such apparently unexceptionable and orthodox assertions as, for example, that of C. S. Lewis, when he claimed that 'all theology would reject the idea of a transaction in which a creature was the agent and God the patient'.[9] God is eternally agent, but the relative independence of his created world points to an element of passivity too within his creative action. We have found ourselves speaking of the suffering of God. And if we are to do full justice to the realities of the world and of human freedom, I confess that I do not see that we can speak otherwise. There are, of course, other courses open to us. We can abandon belief in God. We can interpret our sense of dependence on God in a way that makes it misleading, if not fallacious, to speak of God's creation of the world and of his activity within the world. We can deny the ultimacy of the concept of God and seek something even more ultimate in the concept of an Absolute which embraces nature, man and God. Or we can reaffirm the unqualified transcendence of God, his timelessness and changelessness, by using the impersonal language of a realm of subsisting values or ideas. But none of these alternatives does justice to the specifically Christian insights and assertions, its doctrines of creation and redemption, of incarnation and consummation.

If we persist in our present line of argument, we must reckon seriously with the objection that we have thereby removed the ground from beneath the religious conviction that all things fall not only under the unceasing love of God but also under his unfailing power. The doctrine of divine omnipotence is not lightly to be dismissed. The believer, it is argued, will not be satisfied unless he is assured of an eternal reality which is unthreatened by the contingencies of space and time, of a divine power by which all eventuali-

[9] C. S. Lewis, *Letters to Malcolm*, London 1964, p. 70.

ties are over-ruled. He aspires to a divine peace which is unbroken by the conflicts and anxieties of the world. His God must be above and beyond all change and chance—ultimate, impassible, unlimited. All this, it is urged, belongs to the heart of his faith. It is of the essence of his religion.

Thus far, in broad outline, we may feel disposed to agree. The nub of the objection, however, lies in the further contention that all this is irretrievably lost if we are willing to speak of a God who suffers in and with his world, who is implicated in the conditions which threaten to destroy man's own being, the very conditions which prompt him in the first place to turn to God for salvation. Far from being able to save to the uttermost, a suffering God is no God at all.

Is there any escape from the horns of this dilemma? If God is God, it seems that he must be transcendent, unlimited, impassible. If he is also creator, redeemer and sanctifier, immanent in the moral aspirations and endeavours of his human creatures, it seems that he must be in some respects be limited, even passible. If we are to be faithful to Christian insight, it seems that we cannot give up either of these two convictions. Yet how can we possibly hold on to both?

There is no going back on the ultimacy and transcendence of God. This is basic to our whole concept of God. Granted that this is so, we are left with three possibilities.

In the first place we might abandon the whole notion of the personal involvement of God in the world. Accepting the arguments of Phillips, to which we have referred in an earlier lecture, we might sever the cord with which we have attempted to bind together religion and moral endeavour. We might argue that there can be nothing but confusion if we fail to distinguish and separate the language of moral activity and the language of religious acceptance, and that it is a cardinal error to speak in terms of the purposes of God and to seek in his creative will the ultimate explanation of the world. We might point to self-sacrifice as the hall-mark of a truly religious dependence on God, and from this vantage-point we might proceed to define our peculiarly religious notions of divine transcendence and omnipotence. Certainly such an approach has its attractions. The dilemma disappears. Where the self with its desires and needs is consistently sacrificed, a divine peace may ensue, a peace which nothing can disturb because everything is accepted. If it is possible for a man to achieve this total self-sacrifice, then God may be said to be omnipotent, for no eventuality can prevent this religious response. Whatever happens in the world, good or ill, health or sickness, life or death, a man may accept it through self-negation. Despite its attractions, however, we have resisted the temptation to go along this road. Religion and morality are not to be thus divorced. Endeavour and self-surrender are not to be put asunder. Religious acceptance is an acceptance which walks hand in hand with moral action. Religious sacrifice is a sacrifice which envisages ultimate fulfilment. Religious peace is a peace which anticipates final victory rather than the peace of the non-combatant.

In the second place we might simply assert that we have to retain side by side without reconciliation the contradictory notions of the impassibility and possibility of God. God transcends the world of space and time, he is perfect, unchangeable, eternal. At the same time he is creator, sustainer and redeemer of the world, immanent in its processes and provident of its direction. The obligation which we must accept is to be faithful to the full richness of the religious experience. We must not fail to do justice to its many-sided complexity merely in order to achieve some neat and coherent intellectual system. The divine being will always exceed our intellectual grasp, and it is a mark of honesty and wisdom rather than of folly and deceit to rest in paradox when the facts demand it. After all, other disciplines do not hesitate to make use of complementary but incompatible models when they are needed to give account of the full range of the facts under scrutiny. Why, then, should not theology resort to paradox and even to antinomy if that is what the facts of religious experience require?

For a striking example of such a use of antinomy we may turn once again to Thomas Traherne, who does not hesitate in poetic style to speak in one and the same breath of the wants of the divine love as well as of its perfections: 'The Heathen DEITIES wanted nothing, and were therefore unhappy, for they had no Being. But the LORD GOD of

Israel, the Living and True GOD, was from all Eternity, and from all Eternity Wanted like a GOD. He Wanted the Communication of His Divine Essence, and Persons to Enjoy it. He Wanted Worlds, He wanted Spectators, He wanted Joys, He wanted Treasures. He wanted, yet He wanted not, for He had them.

'This is very strange that GOD should Want. For in Him is the fulness of all Blessedness: He overfloweth Eternally. His Wants are as Glorious as Infinite: Perfective Needs that are in His Nature, and ever Blessed, because always Satisfied. He is from Eternity full of Want, or else He would not be full of Treasure. Infinite Want is the very Ground and Cause of Infinite Treasure. It is Incredible, yet very Plain. Want is the fountain of all His fulness. Want in GOD is treasure to us. For had there been no Need He would not have Created the World, nor made us, nor Manifested His Wisdom, nor Exercised His Power, nor Beautified Eternity, nor prepared the Joys of Heaven. But He wanted Angels and Man, Images, Companions: And these He had from all Eternitie.'[10] In describing the love of God Traherne speaks of his longing to create other beings on whom he may bestow his love, while in describing the perfection of God he speaks as if these beings already shared in the divine eternity. Such use of paradox, 'incredible' and self-contradictory as it may appear, would meet with the qualified approval of many theologians. The human mind can react no further than this antinomy. It must be content with ultimate mystery. Thus we find D. M. Baillie ending his discussion of the very problem with which we ourselves are here concerned with the following words: 'We must be neither too impatient of antinomy nor too tolerant of it, if we are to advance to a clearer understanding of the deep Christian secret. Yet it is not altogether by thinking the matter out, but rather by living it out in daily Christian faith and love, that we shall arrive at a deeper insight in which the paradox will be less acute. And a book about faith cannot end better than upon this note of hope and expectation.'[11] Life is larger than understanding. We must not expect everything in this world to be clear. But we may live in the sure hope that one day we shall know as now we are known.

[10] T. Traherne, *op. cit.*, pp. 79f.   [11] D. M. Baillie, *Faith in God*, p. 301.

While having considerable sympathy with Baillie's conclusion, we may wonder whether the discussion cannot be taken a stage further. Is there not a third course open to us? Can we discern some sort of hierarchy among the analogies which we use to describe the being of God? The antinomy with which we are confronted is basically an antinomy between personal and impersonal analogies. On the one hand the transcendence of God seems best expressed by the impersonal analogies of timelessness, impassibility and universality. On the other hand the immanence of God seems to call for the personal analogies of temporality, involvement and particularity. Is it possible to retain the essential insights of both, while subordinating the one group of analogies to the other?

It should be fairly obvious by now that our own inclination is to stretch to its fullest extent the analogy of personal being, and to see how far we can include in such language all that we wish to say about God before we confront ultimate mystery and rest in silence. Now the fundamental Christian affirmation that God is Love itself makes use of a personal analogy. We may concede that the assertion that God is Love is not equivalent to the assertion that God is loving, but it is certainly not a statement about an abstract idea or ideal such as friendship or justice. God, it is claimed, is a living, active God. It is sometimes said, indeed, that God is more than personal. We need not cavil at this remark if it is intended to remind us that our knowledge of personal being is derived from our own existence, and that we are men and God is God. All the same, we ought to be extremely chary of introducing quasi-impersonal concepts into our discourse about God at the point at which we are exploring the analogy of personal being.

So we return to the concept of personal being, and ask what are the implications of its consistent application to the being of God. What follows is no more than suggestion, a kind of Platonic myth setting out something of what the truth may be like.

The concept of personal being involves the concepts of freedom, activity and relationship. These, it seems to me, also involve the concept of time, of a movement from the living present into the yet unrealized future. It looks, then, as if we must be prepared in some way to apply temporal categories to God. Eternal though he is, his eternity is admittedly not the timelessness of abstract ideas. But do we make any progress in our thought if we claim that it is a timelessness in which, in a single intuitive grasp, God knows what is for us the unborn and non-existent future in much the same way as one might comprehend the once living but now dead past? On the other hand, time has traditionally been considered to be an aspect of creatureliness and finitude, a mark of imperfection and instability, of coming into being and passing away. Consequently, there has been a *consensus* of theological opinion that temporal characteristics must in no way be ascribed to God. He is beyond time. He does not come into being or pass away. He eternally is.

The suggestion that I wish to make is this. While some of the characteristics of our temporal, personal being are certainly marks of our finitude and imperfection, temporality as such is not itself a mark of imperfection. In employing the analogy of personal being in order to speak of God, we may therefore try to remove the imperfections inherent in our own being without at the same time doing away altogether with the notion of temporality.

Now our experience of our own personal being reveals two obvious imperfections. First, we are what we are to a large extent because of what our heredity and environment have made us. Our freedom is limited by those very conditions which our nature imposes upon us. Second, we experience a dichotomy between what we are as persons and what we know we ought to be. We are continually falling short of the authentic being which we know to be our proper heritage into various forms of inauthentic being. It is possible, however, to conceive of God without these two imperfections.

God has no nature other than his own personal being. He is not essentially limited 'from outside'. He does not come into being, nor will he go out of being. He simply is, ultimate and eternal. It is, however, of his essence to love and to impart himself by loving. His eternal being realizes itself in unceasing activity. There is both an eternal fount of love and a continuing expression of love.

Love given fulfils itself in love received. We may, then, go on to posit some kind of relation within the unity of the Godhead. The

Father begets the Son and the Son returns the Father's love in a perfect interpenetration of personal being. Perfect unity embraces perfect relationship because the relationship is personal. It is a relationship in the Spirit. If this is the case, it might be argued that the creation of a finite world is not necessary to the being of God. It is an ultimate contingency. God would still be God, were there no finite world. Such, for example, is the view of Barth. He distinguishes between the doctrine of predestination and the doctrine of providence as follows: 'The root of the doctrine of predestination is to be found in the being of God. But the doctrine of providence has no corresponding root of which this may be said. On the presupposition of the finished work of creation and the given existence of the creature we can certainly say that as Creator God would be untrue to Himself in this relationship with His creature without the knowing, willing and acting described in the doctrine of providence. But He would be no less God even if the work of creation had never been done, if there were no creatures, and if the whole doctrine of providence was therefore irrelevant.'[12] Alternatively, it might be argued that creativity is essential to the divine Being, and that the work of creation expresses that element of 'co-operation' which we have detected in personal being. There is participation and confrontation within the Godhead; there is also a divine co-operation in the work of creation. The contingency of this world is preserved because there was no divine necessity to create *this* world. But there was a divine necessity to create *a* world. Love issues in creation. The very perfection of God expresses itself in a work to be perfected. Becoming has its root in Being.

In any case, the finite world exists. God has freely created the world of which we are part. As the creation of Love it has both an ultimate dependence on God and a relative independence of its own. We cannot give much positive content to the notion of the divine creation *ex nihilo*. The nearest that we can get to it, perhaps, is in our human experience of being the recipients of a love which gives us, as it were out of nothing, a personal being of our own. Nor need we say that ours is 'the best of all possible worlds'; only that

[12] K. Barth, *Church Dogmatics, III*, 3, p. 5.

it is one of many possible worlds which would express the divine love and creativity. God's love is perfect and unchanging; but the created objects of his love, and consequently his relations with them, do change. His love is infinitely variable but infinitely reliable. He is enriched by the responding love of his creatures, but he himself is the ultimate source of their love, and this enrichment of the divine love is a mark of its perfection, not of its imperfection. We might put the matter in this way: that while God's love is perfect, his joy increases.

There is, then, a distinction to be made within the being of God. There is the love by which he posits himself. He cannot not love. There is also his creativity. Love eternally creates new objects for its love and finds new expressions of its love. Creativity is an activity of divine personal being. In God time is the measure, not of change and decay, but of perfection. In him time is fulfilled, not abrogated. Because personal being is inconceivable without activity and temporality, we are not precluded from using personal analogies in speaking of the perfect being of God.

The value of impersonal analogies lies, as we have seen, in their suggestion of unchanging universality, that of personal analogies in their suggestion of active creativity. Both insights, however, can be preserved if we retain as fundamental the personal analogies. Furthermore, in so far as the divine love is fulfilled in response, it is proper to speak also of God's receptivity. In all love there is a giving and receiving. No exception need be made of the love of God. And given the fact of a finite and created world, in regard to which we are compelled to speak of the suffering of God, we wish to affirm that such suffering is not an imperfection, although it is admittedly a limitation, because it reflects a receptivity which is fundamental to the perfection of God's own being.

Although we may have done something towards removing the antimony between eternity and time, between the transcendent changelessness of God and his immanent activity in the world, and have argued that both are aspects of his perfect being, we have not fully answered the question whether religious confidence in the outcome of Love's creative venture is or is not misplaced.

What are the consequences of the view we have been adumbrating for faith in God's 'never-failing providence'? How can we be so sure that his purposes will not fail? Can we commit ourselves and our ways to him with complete and utter confidence that they are in safe keeping?

The answer we shall give to these questions will depend upon our understanding of the strength and weakness of perfect Love. We may be sure that everything has its ultimate source and origin in Love. We may be sure that nothing, so to speak, will take it by surprise. As God is the creative ground not only of this actual world but of all possible worlds, there is no possibility which might somehow have escaped his divine forethought. We may be equally sure that nothing can be beyond the reach of Love. We may also put our trust in its ultimacy, constancy, persistency and patience. What we shall not be able to do is at some point to abandon our faith in the primacy of Love and seek a false security in some totally different concept of naked power. Faith in God's providence and hope in God's future will always remain a venture. Neither permits of conclusive demonstration. The tragedy that threatens to break man's spirit and destroy his world is a constant reminder of Love's weakness. But faith also apprehends Love's strength and gives to hope a logic of its own. The Christian apprehends God's working preeminently in the life, death and resurrection of Jesus Christ, and in him it discerns God's weakness and God's strength. Here is Love that suffers, but here also is Love that triumphs. Tragedy itself, accepted, endured, transfigured and redeemed, ministers to a new and richer life. Sin, suffering and death are woven into the pattern of divine providence. Contrary to his will they are rendered subservient to his will. So faith discerns, and hope is renewed. Love will have its perfect way. God's kingdom is, and is to come. 'It behoved that there should be sin; but all shall be well, and all shall be well, and all manner of thing shall be well.'[13]

[13] Julian of Norwich, *Revelations of Divine Love*, ed. Grace Warrack, London n.d., p. 56.